The Mental Health Tribunal

Sara Miller McCune founded SAGE Publishing in 1965 to support the dissemination of usable knowledge and educate a global community. SAGE publishes more than 1000 journals and over 800 new books each year, spanning a wide range of subject areas. Our growing selection of library products includes archives, data, case studies and video. SAGE remains majority owned by our founder and after her lifetime will become owned by a charitable trust that secures the company's continued independence.

Los Angeles | London | New Delhi | Singapore | Washington DC | Melbourne

The Mental Health Tribunal

An Essential Guide

NEIL HICKMAN and CHRISTINE HUTCHISON

Learning Matters
A SAGE Publishing Company
1 Oliver's Yard
55 City Road
London EC1Y 1SP

SAGE Publications Inc.
2455 Teller Road
Thousand Oaks, California 91320

SAGE Publications India Pvt Ltd
B 1/I 1 Mohan Cooperative Industrial Area
Mathura Road
New Delhi 110 044

SAGE Publications Asia-Pacific Pte Ltd
3 Church Street
#10-04 Samsung Hub
Singapore 049483

Editor: Kate Keers
Development editor: Sarah Turpie
Senior project editor: Chris Marke
Project management: River Editorial
Marketing manager: Camille Richmond
Cover design: Wendy Scott
Typeset by: C&M Digitals (P) Ltd, Chennai, India
Printed in the UK

Library of Congress Control Number: 2021942041

British Library Cataloguing in Publication Data

A catalogue record for this book is available from the British Library

ISBN 978-1-5297-0850-9
ISBN 978-1-5297-0849-3 (pbk)

At SAGE we take sustainability seriously. Most of our products are printed in the UK using responsibly sourced papers and boards. When we print overseas we ensure sustainable papers are used as measured by the PREPS grading system. We undertake an annual audit to monitor our sustainability.

Contents

Acknowledgements

We are indebted to the colleagues and clients we have worked alongside in the course of our careers.

It would not have been possible to write this book without the assistance and support of those both attending the Tribunal and those on the Tribunal Panel. We are also grateful for the many experiences and questions raised by participants on training courses. This has, we hope, shaped the book and offered some answers to those tricky practice questions.

In particular we would like to thank the following people who have kindly offered advice, read various drafts and pointed us in the right direction, also offering information on differences between the English and Welsh systems and rules.

We would like to thank Kate Akester, Dr Lorraine Ashman, Nigel Butcher, Andy Coombs, Dr Jonathan Cripps, Dr David Firth, Tam Gill, Rosalind Green and team, Hazel Mackay, Margaret Modeste, Lisa Moylan, Dr Camilla Parker, Russell Parkes, Sunni Webb and Jonathan Wilson.

And, of course, a special thank you to Sarah Turpie, Development Editor, for her patience and ceaseless support with our many passed deadlines and Kate Keers, Senior Commissioning Editor, in particular for her enthusiasm and positive comments at the start of the process, and ongoing optimism and encouragement. Thank you also to Keith Brown, Series Editor, and Catriona McMullen, Associate Editor (Social Work).

This book reflects the law as we believed it to stand on 1 June 2021. Any inaccuracies are ours alone and we take full responsibility for this.

Christine Hutchison
Edge Training and Consultancy Ltd
Neil Hickman
Consultant solicitor
Gledhill Gill Solicitors

About the authors

Christine Hutchison is a registered social worker. She worked in the NHS and several Local Authorities for over 30 years and as an Approved Social Worker/Approved Mental Health Professional (ASW/AMHP) for over 18 years. She has managed mental health services, worked for the Care Quality Commission and lectured on several post-qualifying AMHP university courses. Christine has been a director of Edge Training and Consultancy Ltd since 2013, where she delivers training on mental health and capacity law and practice to health and social care professionals and others. Christine is a Specialist Lay Member of the Mental Health Tribunal (England). Christine has previously published a mental health law book for social workers.

Neil Hickman is a specialist mental health solicitor and a member of the Law Society Mental Health Panel. He also holds a Diploma and Master's in Social Work and previously worked as a mental health social worker (ASW and AMHP) and mental health team manager. He is a visiting lecturer in law at the University of Hertfordshire and also provides post-qualifying legal training to mental health professionals. Neil has previously published a mental health law book for social workers and contributed to a number of research papers.

Foreword from the series editor

This practical guide is written by two professionals with extensive experience of the Tribunal and of working with a range of professionals in different roles, including Judges, Medical Members, Specialist Lay Members, Mental Health Act Administrators, legal representatives, Independent Mental Health Advocates and other professionals who attend hearings.

There are numerous textbooks on Mental Health Tribunal law and procedure for lawyers and Judges and various excellent textbooks for social workers on Court skills. However, as the Mental Health Tribunal is a unique Court, it requires a specific book that can focus on and offer a clear explanation of all stages of the Tribunal proceedings, from initial application through to the final decision.

Clear chapter headings and direct quotations from a range of professionals make it possible to dip in and out of the text for quick reference and insights. In addition to Tribunal work, the authors have significant wider experience of working within mental health services and therefore understand 'real life' experiences. As a result, the text is not overly legalistic or academic and concentrates on developing confidence and good practice in this area of work.

I want to personally thank the authors for their time and skill in producing this text; it will make such a difference to professional practice. Neil Hickman and Christine Hutchison have a wealth of experience of both Tribunals but also the wider legal system and this readable text assists all professionals in both an understanding of and how to work with Tribunals. I warmly recommend it to all working in this area of practice.

Readers will also find this book useful to read in conjunction with another SAGE/Learning Matters text: *Mental Health Law in England and Wales: A Guide for Mental Health Professionals* by Paul Barber, Robert Brown and Debbie Martin.

Professor Keith Brown
Director
The National Centre for Post-Qualifying Social Work
and Professional Practice (NCPQSWPP)
Centre for Leadership, Impact and Management Bournemouth (CLiMB)

Introduction

Why this practical guide and who is it for?

This guide is intended very much as a practical guide rather than a legal text and is aimed primarily at busy mental health and social care professionals preparing reports for and attending Tribunals to give oral evidence. It covers the law as it applies to the Mental Health Tribunal in England (MHT) and Mental Health Review Tribunal for Wales (MHRTW). We have used the term 'Tribunal' throughout the book to cover both the English and Welsh systems. The law is different in Scotland and in Ireland and is not covered in this book.

Written by two experienced trainers: a lawyer who represents patients in Tribunal proceedings and a social worker who is also a Specialist Lay Member of the Tribunal. The book aims to demystify Tribunal proceedings, offering clear and accurate explanations throughout.

It should also prove helpful to others who support patients in the Tribunal process, including Mental Health Act Administrators and Managers, advocacy services and the private and voluntary sector. Patients and their families might also find the explanations of Tribunal processes helpful.

Tribunals can cause anxiety for professionals, patients and families, particularly the inexperienced or uninitiated. Many professionals tell us they are asked to prepare and present reports with no advance training or understanding of what the Tribunal is or what it can do. They are therefore underprepared and misunderstand what is expected of them, which can lead to unnecessarily stressful and difficult experiences at Tribunal hearings. This book will guide them through the process from advance planning, the Tribunal hearing itself, what happens after the hearing and how to ensure the welfare of the patient.

What will it include and what is not included?

The book does not provide a critical analysis of the Tribunal system or explore the merits of one legal system over another. Whether or not readers have found it an effective or efficient process in practice or whether or not it might take on a wider role, as proposed in the Government's white paper Reforming the Mental Health Act (Department of Health and Social Care, 2021) are not issues that this practical guide explores.

However, it does offer explanation and guidance on the role of the Tribunal in considering the Mental Capacity Act 2005 (MCA) and its interface with the Mental Health Act 1983 (MHA). Case-law specific to capacity and its application to the Tribunal will be integrated into the text.

As this is not a legal text, the reader will find a number of excellent books in the bibliography dealing with the legal detail of the Tribunal proceedings should they wish to have a deeper knowledge of the relevant statutory provisions and case-law. We have tried to avoid clogging the text with extensive legal referencing; however, readers wishing to find source materials will find the relevant information within the referencing, table of cases and table of statutory materials.

Continuing professional development

Mental health nurses, occupational therapists, psychologists, psychiatrists, social workers and anyone studying in these professions should find this text assists them in their continuing professional development. For example, those training as Approved Mental Health Professionals (AMHPs) will be required to meet specific regulatory requirements and competencies, including the ability to present a case at a legal hearing. Those seeking Approved Clinician status will be required to show the ability to present evidence to Courts and Tribunals.

Layout of book and some additional resources in appendices

The learning features in the book are intended to assist busy professionals to understand how the Tribunal works in practice. These include 'Top tips' for each chapter and 'Frequently asked questions and answers'. There are short activity boxes within the chapters that can be used for training purposes to consolidate learning and apply theory and law to practice. In the course of writing this book we have had the benefit and privilege of receiving contributions from some hugely experienced Tribunal Members and mental health lawyers and you will find quotes from these experts throughout the book. Finally, at the end of each chapter, key points are summarised.

The book sets the scene by offering a brief history of the development of the Tribunal and setting out the legal context in which the Tribunal operates. It then follows the process from who can apply and when; to what the Tribunal can and cannot do; the role of the Tribunal Panel Members and who is expected to attend and give oral evidence. It offers practical assistance in the writing of reports and giving oral evidence, including how to deal with questions from the Panel and cross-examination by the legal representative.

There will be explanations for what happens before a hearing and issues such as how to manage a request to withhold information or how to assist a patient who is deemed to lack the capacity to instruct a legal representative.

There is a chapter dedicated to the welfare of the patient and how to manage the process in a manner that does not exclude or isolate them.

The mechanisms for challenging Tribunal decisions and for making complaints are explained at the end of the book.

Differences between England and Wales

Although the MHA 1983 applies to England and Wales, there are some aspects of mental health law that vary between the two countries. England and Wales have separate MHA Codes of Practice and the Welsh Assembly has devolved powers to make 'Measures', in other words law, that apply only to Wales. For example, the Mental Health (Wales) Measure 2010 Part 2 covers duties to provide care and treatment planning and care coordination. The equivalent in England at the time of writing is the Care Programme Approach (CPA), which is policy rather than law.

Although the Tribunal system originated in the 1959 Mental Health Act for England and Wales, in 2007 the two systems separated. In England, the Tribunal system became part of a wider Tribunal system under the Tribunals, Courts and Enforcement Act 2007 and was renamed the First-tier Tribunal (Mental Health). In Wales, the Mental Health Review Tribunal for Wales remains established under Part V of the MHA 1983. We will explain any key differences between England and Wales within the text.

Legal terminology and abbreviations used within the text

Complex terms are explained within the text. Otherwise, we refer you to the glossary.

Any references to particular sections, e.g. 's.2' are to the Mental Health Act 1983 unless otherwise stated.

Unless otherwise stated, references to 'Codes' are to the Mental Health Act 1983 Code of Practice 2015 for England and the Mental Health Act 1983 Code of Practice 2016 for Wales.

Similarly, unless otherwise stated, any references to 'Rules' are to the Tribunal (First-tier Tribunal) (Health, Education and Social Care Chamber) Procedure Rules 2008 (for England) and the Mental Health Review Tribunal for Wales Rules 2008. References to Practice Directions (PDs) are to the Practice Direction First-tier Tribunal: Statements and Reports in Mental Health Cases 2013 and the Mental Health Review Tribunal for Wales Practice Direction: Statements and Reports for Mental Health Review Tribunals in Wales 2019. For brevity of referencing you will see '(E)' for England and '(W)' Wales if there are any differences in the Codes, Rules or Practice Directions.

For simplicity, we have used the term Responsible Clinician (RC) throughout the book. In most cases, this will be the Consultant Psychiatrist responsible for the treatment of a patient subject to the Mental Health Act but could be a non-medical professional. The Practice Directions require reports to be written, or countersigned by the RC. We acknowledge that, in practice, writing reports and attendance at Tribunal hearings will not necessarily be done by the RC and will be undertaken by doctors at different stages of training. There is a helpful guidance document produced by the Tribunal and Royal College of Psychiatrists, which can be accessed here:

www.rcpsych.ac.uk/docs/default-source/training/curricula-and-guidance/curricula-guidance-for-detaining-authorities-about-medical-evidence-first-tier-Tribunal.pdf?sfvrsn=923126b_2

Finally, we have used the term 'Care Coordinator' throughout the book to denote the mental health professional from community services with the primary responsibility for arranging care and treatment for patients in the community. We are aware that some areas now use alternative terms such as 'Lead Practitioner'.

Finally, because we anticipate that this is a book that professionals may dip into, we have explained any abbreviations upon first use in every chapter.

The coronavirus pandemic

The writing of this book spanned 2020 and the early months of 2021 and therefore coincided with the extraordinary social upheaval brought about by the pandemic, which had a seismic impact on mental health services and professionals, the delivery of care and treatment and, of course, on patients. The operation of the Tribunal system changed dramatically from the point of the first lockdown on 23 March 2020: face-to-face hearings were suspended; pre-hearing examinations by the Medical Member of the Tribunal were suspended due to becoming impracticable; Community Treatment Order hearings in England were suspended for a short period; the whole Tribunal process immediately became 'remote'; and hearings were initially conducted as telephone conferences. In England, telephone hearings were initially conducted by single-Judge Panels (with access to Medical and Specialist Lay Members for consultation if needed) before returning to full Panels, while telephone hearings with full Panels continued in Wales. In England, s.2 patients, recalled conditionally discharged patients and child and adolescent cases were prioritised. Alongside this, patients lost or had significantly reduced opportunities to have face-to-face contact with their families, their community mental health teams, their legal representatives and IMHAs. Section 17 leave was intermittently suspended and transition to community placements became very difficult during the lockdowns, which had a major impact on patients' progression along their care pathways towards discharge.

A raft of legislative changes, rule changes, emergency Practice Directions and guidance documents were issued in response to the rapidly changing picture and, on reflection, the lack of any significant delay in patients having their cases heard (at least in some form) was a remarkable achievement by the Tribunal services, hospitals and other stakeholders. Even more remarkable in our experience has been the way that patients have coped so admirably with this major change to Tribunal procedure and the way that their cases were heard.

As we all adjusted and became ever more familiar with the creative use of technology, in England, Tribunal proceedings progressed to video conference hearings with full Panels by July 2020, and it became possible to request a pre-hearing examination (PHE) with the Medical Member by video-link if practicable. It became apparent that all cases were being dealt with without the need for any prioritisation. At the time of writing, in Wales, hearings continue to be conducted by telephone conference and pre-hearing examinations are still deemed to be impracticable. We understand that, following a successful legal challenge, a trial of video hearings is now to take place in Wales.

Remote hearings have presented a challenge to all concerned with the inevitable technological glitches and the difficulties for the Tribunal and others being unable to 'read the room', making it difficult to assess how a patient is coping with the hearing or how they might react to a negative decision. In England, this issue is dealt with case by case, with some decisions being given on the day via the video-link and others being emailed to the parties later. In Wales, decisions are always delivered by email the following working day.

We thought very carefully about whether or not to incorporate these issues and changes to the Tribunal process into the main body of the text but decided not to for three reasons: first, most of the information and guidance in the book is as applicable to telephone or video hearings as it is to face-to-face hearings; second, the rate of change of policy and practice as the crisis has ebbed and flowed has been rapid, and we suspect will be subject to further changes as things progress. An attempt to capture the situation at a particular moment in time is destined to be very quickly out-of-date. Third, we hope, of course, that in the near future Tribunal practice and procedure will return to something resembling the pre-pandemic position, although we suspect that the skills and knowledge accumulated by all concerned in the use of technology may mean that some aspects of this might remain after the crisis is behind us.

For those interested in the detail, Mental Health Law Online has catalogued all of the relevant rules, Practice Directions and legal changes and guidance that have been issued in the course of the pandemic. It is very comprehensive and will become a remarkable legal artefact of the crisis (see www.mentalhealthlaw.co.uk/Coronavirus_resources).

Book overview

If you have a specific question, you should be able to dip in and out of the relevant chapters and there are cross-references if the information is also covered elsewhere.

Chapter 1: History and legal context

This chapter demystifies the Tribunal and explains that it is a specialised Court for which professionals and others need to be appropriately prepared. It offers pictorial guides to show the structure of the Tribunal within the Court system. There is also clarification of what a Hospital Managers review is and the Hospital Managers' power of discharge.

Chapter 2: Applications and references to the Tribunal

For those who need to know when patients and Nearest Relatives can apply to the Tribunal and when a reference will be made to the Tribunal. We have included a handy table that sets out timescales clearly and can be used as a checklist. There is a discussion of capacity issues as they might apply to the Tribunal process.

Chapter 3: What powers and duties does the Tribunal have?

Here we explain the range of powers and duties the Tribunal has and the possible outcomes of a hearing, including discharge of the patient.

Chapter 4: Who is on the Tribunal Panel and what are their roles?

The role, specialisms and qualifications of each Tribunal Panel Member are explained.

Chapter 5: Who should attend the Tribunal hearing and why?

Professionals should be aware of when they should or must attend a hearing. The Tribunal decides who should attend, and has the power to direct attendance or to exclude a person from a hearing. This chapter answers frequently asked questions, including what to do if the author of a report cannot attend the Tribunal.

Chapter 6: How do Tribunals apply the law?

Here we set out the legal tests and likely lines of questioning by the Panel and patient's representative. We explain the key terminology used, for example, 'statutory criteria', 'mental disorder', 'nature', 'degree' and the commonly termed 'risk criteria'. Understanding the statutory criteria should assist the reader in their preparations for report writing and managing their oral evidence at the hearing.

Chapters 7: Preparing written evidence

Essential reading for those who are preparing a report for the Tribunal. We look at general requirements for all Tribunal reports before looking in more detail at the reports written by the:

- Responsible Clinician (RC);
- Inpatient nurse; and
- Social circumstances report (SCR) author.

We explain the 'Practice Direction' headings and focus on the trickier headings to offer guidance on what is required of authors. We also explain what to do if the author wishes to withhold information from the patient.

Chapter 8: Pre-hearing matters

For those who are curious about what happens behind the scenes before the actual hearing starts. We cover what can happen between the initial application or reference and the hearing itself. We explain timescales and why professionals might be chased for their availability or for reports.

Chapter 9: What happens at the hearing?

Is the hearing public or private? What is the Panel doing before the hearing starts? Why is the start time sometimes delayed? Why does the hearing not go ahead having come this far? Who speaks first, asks questions and in what order? What questions are likely to be asked of professionals? These questions are answered and the hearing procedure explained.

Chapter 10: The welfare of the patient

It is important to bear in mind how a hearing might impact on the patient and their relationships with professionals, carers and family. This chapter offers advice on how to support patients before, during and after a Tribunal hearing.

Chapter 11: Decisions, reviews and appeals

What happens after the hearing and in what circumstances can the decision of the Tribunal be challenged? What steps can be taken if there is a concern about the conduct of a Panel Member or legal representative at a hearing?

Chapter 1
History and legal context

Introduction

This chapter will provide an overview of what the Tribunal is, why they exist and the interface with human rights. There is also a short explanation of the role of the Hospital Managers in reviewing a patient's detention and how these differ from the Tribunal.

What is a Mental Health (Review) Tribunal?

In simple terms, the Tribunal's role is to review whether a patient should remain subject to the Mental Health Act (MHA), with the most important power being to discharge the patient from detention or community compulsion (patients subject to Community Treatment Orders (CTOs), Guardianship or conditional discharge). Most patients subject to detention in hospital or compulsion in the community are entitled to apply to have their case heard by the Tribunal, with the exceptions that generally patients subject to short-term emergency or holding powers and patients subject to interim orders or remands from the criminal Courts are not eligible to apply to the Tribunal.

As well as the power to discharge, the Tribunal has additional powers (discussed in detail in Chapter 3) but have no powers to regulate the conditions of detention (*Djaba v West London MH Trust* [2017]), or consider the validity of the initial detention or compulsion (*R v East London and the City MH Trust Ex p Brandenburg* [2003]) and no powers over the specifics of a treatment regime (*SH v Cornwall Partnership NHS Trust* [2012]).

The Tribunal has been described as an '*independent judicial body*' (MHA Code 12.2 (E and W)). Many of the common mistakes made by professionals could be avoided by understanding that they are providing written and oral evidence in Court. This can come as a surprise to those attending a Tribunal hearing due to the perceived informality of the proceedings. The informality and itinerant nature of the hearings is entirely to meet the needs of patients. They aim to be accessible and the overriding objective within the Tribunal's Rules (Rule 2 (E), Rule 3 (W)) is to deal with cases fairly and justly, which includes avoiding unnecessary formality, avoiding delay and enabling participation. This is why timescales can seem tight to professionals and why deadlines for reports are required.

> *EXPERT QUOTE*
>
> *It is a Court of law – facts, evidence, law. Be familiar with these three factors, and you will be in a stronger position and feel more confident and be more enabled to give good evidence.*

We look at the roles of the Tribunal Panel Members in more detail in Chapter 4.

Development of the Tribunal system

Historically, mental health law required judicial scrutiny ('certification') *before* admission to hospital. The 1959 Mental Health Act removed this requirement with provisions for a Mental Welfare Officer (the ancestor to the current Approved Mental Health Professional (AMHP)) to apply for detention in hospital on the basis of medical recommendations without recourse to a Court. The Mental Health Review Tribunal (MHRT) (England and Wales) was also established under the 1959 Act to provide the required judicial scrutiny *after* the initial admission or reception into Guardianship.

In 1950 the UK became the first signatory to the European Convention for the Protection of Human Rights and Fundamental Freedoms (ECHR). The newly established MHRT in the 1959 Act complied with the rights of individuals to have their case heard speedily by an impartial Court with the power to order their discharge (Article 5(4) ECHR).

As the MHA Code (12.4 (E), 12.3 (W)) states, the Tribunal 'provides a significant safeguard for patients who have had their liberty curtailed under the Act'.

Prior to the MHA 1959, there was no specialist Tribunal system by which patients could challenge their detention. The only legal mechanism available to a patient would be to apply to Court for a writ of habeas corpus (an ancient legal procedure whereby the authorities detaining a person are required to attend Court to justify the lawfulness of the detention).

Table 1.1   Brief history of relevant mental health law and safeguards

1215: Magna Carta	*'...No freeman ought to be taken, or imprisoned or disseized of his freehold, liberties or privileges, or outlawed, or exiled, or in any manner destroyed, or deprived of his life, liberty or property, but by judgment of his peers, or by the law of the land'.*
1890: Lunacy Act	Between 1300 and 1800 there were various legal provisions for the poor, destitute and mentally ill.
	In 1890 the Lunacy Act required the Magistrate or County Court Judge to certify detention in a public asylum on the basis of doctors' recommendations.

1930: Mental Treatment Act	Voluntary admission was possible without any requirement for certification via the Courts.
1949: Legal Aid Act	Although this introduced legal aid, it was not widely available until the 1970s. Initially, Tribunal hearings under the 1959 Act would often be without legal representation for the client.
1950: European Convention on Human Rights (ECHR)	See later for details of the ECHR right to liberty, right to a fair trial and right to respect for private and family life.
1959 Mental Health Act	A radical overhaul of mental health law, repealing all previous legislation dealing with the mentally disordered. The 1959 MHA *still provides the basic framework of modern English mental health legislation'* (Hale, 2017).
	Significantly, it dispensed with the certification process for civil admissions. Instead of Court involvement at initial admission, doctors made recommendations and a social worker (Mental Welfare Officer) or relative could make applications for admission.
	As Article 5(4) ECHR required a speedy review of any deprivation of liberty and its lawfulness the MHRT was developed to provide judicial oversight with the power to order discharge.
1983: Mental Health Act	Following a review of the 1959 Act, the 1983 Act kept much that had gone before. Safeguards for patients were improved including increased access to the Tribunal.
1998: Human Rights Act	ECHR rights are incorporated in to UK domestic law.
2005: Mental Capacity Act	Part VII of the MHA 1983 dealing with the personal welfare, property and financial affairs of patients was repealed by the Mental Capacity Act 2005 which also established a new Court of Protection.
2007: Mental Health Act	This amended the existing 1983 Act. The 1983 Act has been subject to various amendments. For example, the Mental Health (Patients in the Community) Act 1995 amended the 1983 MHA to make provision for supervised discharge under s.25A. The MHA 2007 repealed this and replaced it with CTOs. It is, therefore, entirely correct to continue to refer to it as the MHA 1983. Here are some key amendments made via the 2007 Act:
	• Introduction of a new broad definition of mental disorder in s.1.
	• Introduction of Approved Mental Health Professionals (AMHPs) to replace Approved Social Workers (ASWs) and Responsible Clinicians (RCs) to replace Responsible Medical Officers (RMOs).
	• Introduction of CTOs in s.17A.
	• Inserted the Deprivation of Liberty Safeguards (DoLS) into the MCA (Schedule A1).
	In England the legal establishment of the Tribunal was removed from the MHA and became part of the Tribunals Courts and Enforcement Act 2007 (see below) and is now termed the First-tier Tribunal.

(Continued)

Table 1.1   (Continued)

	In Wales, the Tribunal system remained in the Mental Health Act (Part V, s.65 and Schedule 2) and became the Mental Health Review Tribunal for Wales. Appeals from both Tribunals go to the UK Upper Tribunal (see below). Both Tribunals have the same powers and duties which are in Part V of the MHA. Although they do have separate rules and procedures. More information on both systems can be found at www.mentalhealthreviewtribunal.gov.wales/ and www.judiciary.uk.
Tribunal, Courts and Enforcement Act 2007	This legislation deals with a wide range of other legal areas such as special education needs, social security and child support and asylum support.
Mental Capacity (Amendment) Act 2019	Replacement for Deprivation of Liberty Safeguards. Commonly termed the Liberty Protection Safeguards.

The structure of the Court system

Having emphasised that the Tribunal is a specialised Court, it is worth considering where the Tribunal sits within the overall Court structure of the UK. Below (Figure 1.1) is a very simplified diagram of the civil Court system and hierarchy, including the Tribunal and Upper Tribunal followed by a more detailed diagram of the Tribunal system.

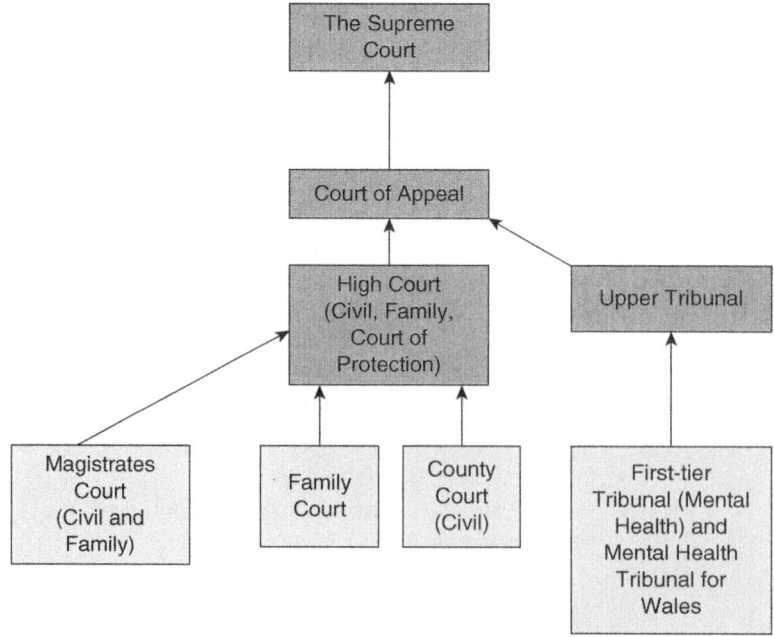

Figure 1.1   Simplified civil Court system

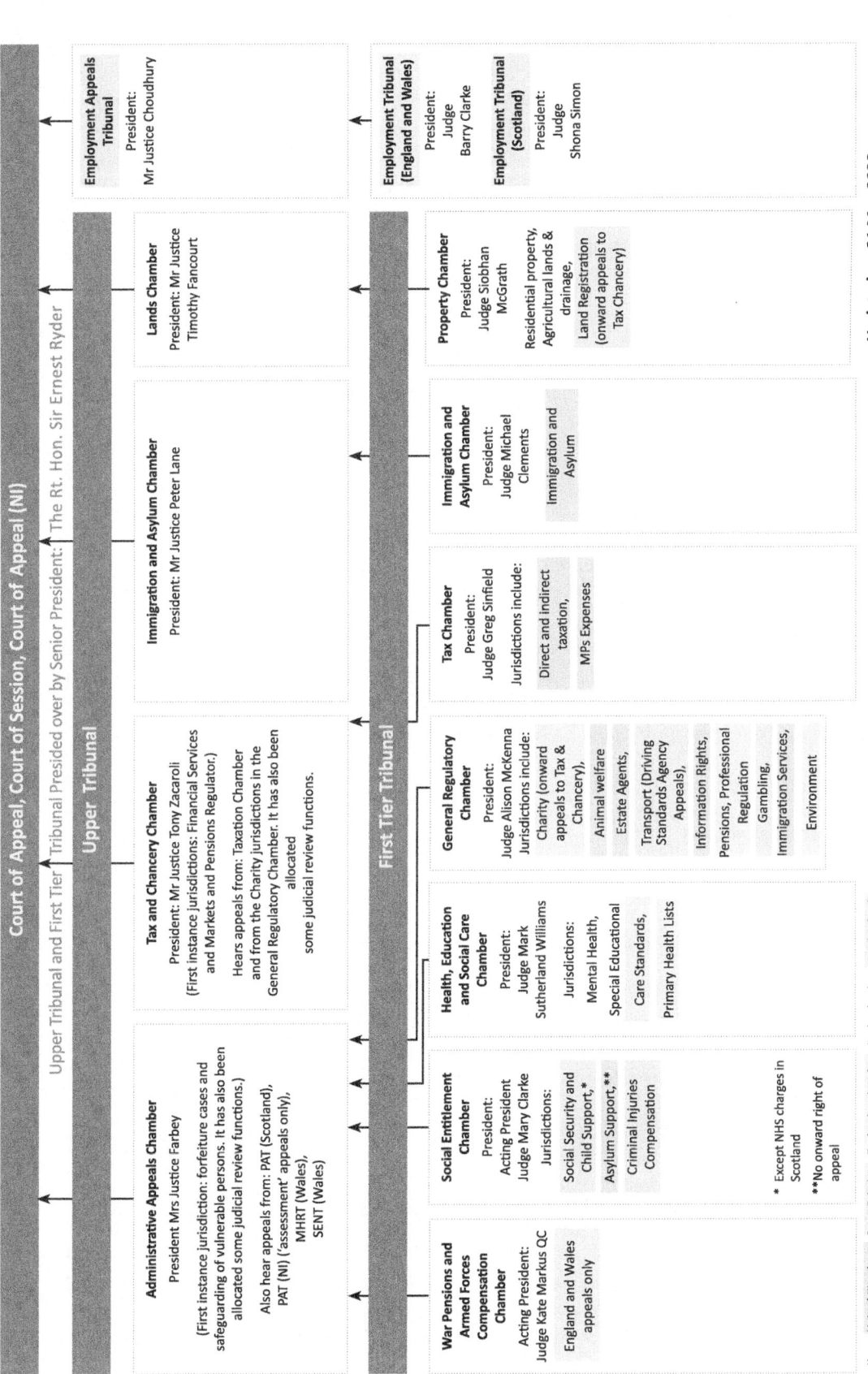

Figure 1.2   Tribunal system (Senior President of Tribunals' Annual Report 2020)

As can be seen in Figure 1.2, the structures of the English and Welsh Tribunal systems vary. In England, there are several chambers, and the First-tier Tribunal for Mental Health sits within the Health Education and Social Care Chamber. Each chamber is overseen by the Senior President of Tribunals and has a President and Deputy President. Below them are the relevant Tribunal Members and Judges. There is a central administration system for the First-tier Tribunal in Mental Health. This is situated in Leicester, and staff are employed by Her Majesty's Court and Tribunal Service (HMCTS) and independent of the hospital. The First-tier Tribunal (Mental Health) can be contacted at:

First-tier Tribunal (Mental Health)

PO Box 8793

5th Floor

Leicester

LE1 8BN

0300-123-2201 or mhtenquiries@justice.gov.uk

The Welsh Mental Health Review Tribunal structure is set out in s.65 MHA and in relevant schedules. There is a central office in Cardiff, dealing with administration and called the Secretariat. This Secretariat and the Tribunal Members are funded by the Welsh Government. However, their workings and decisions are independent of Government and they are overseen by a Tribunal President. The MHRTW can be contacted at:

2nd floor

Crown Buildings

Cathays Park

Cardiff

CF10 3NQ

0300 0255328 or MHRT@gov.wales

In practice, there is little difference between the two Tribunals for those attending a hearing to give evidence.

Tribunal powers, applications and references, legal tests

Part V of the MHA deals with applications and references to the Tribunal, the Tribunal's powers and the legal tests to be applied in Tribunal proceedings (see Chapter 2). There are also detailed procedural rules governing the Tribunal, dealing with matters such as evidence, timescales, appeals and the case management powers available to the Tribunal. These will be explored in detail in Chapter 3.

Appeals, binding decisions and case-law

The darker shaded boxes in Figure 1.1 indicate 'superior' Courts (sometimes referred to as 'Courts of record'), which means that their decisions are binding (must be followed) by any Court at the same level or below in the hierarchy. So, if you look up any recent mental health case-law, the decision will probably have been made by the Upper Tribunal (UKUT), the Court of Appeal (EWCA) or the Supreme Court (UKSC). The Upper Tribunal has taken on roles previously dealt with by the High Court and now sits alongside the High Court and Court of Protection in the hierarchy. The Court of Protection's position is a little more complex as cases can be heard by different levels of Judges, but it is a Court of record.

The arrows indicate the route of appeal against a decision so, for a patient seeking discharge from detention under s.3 MHA, for example, the case will initially be heard by the MHT or MHRTW. If not discharged from detention or compulsion in the community, the patient *might* be able to appeal on an error or point of law to the Upper Tribunal, then the Court of Appeal and then the Supreme Court. This is exactly what occurred in the 'PJ' case (*Welsh Ministers v PJ* [2018]), a case that concerned the conditions that a Responsible Clinician (RC) may or may not impose under a CTO (see Chapter 11 for the details of the case). The right to appeal a Tribunal decision is not absolute: permission is required and the grounds for an appeal are narrow. For example, even to be granted permission to appeal to the Upper Tribunal, the patient would have to show that the decision involved the making of an error on a point of law (s.12(1) Tribunals, Courts and Enforcement Act 2007). The vast majority of applications against detention or compulsion in the community start and end at the Tribunal. For our purposes, the right-hand side of the diagram in Figure 1.1 is the likely legal pathway. Appeals are dealt with in more detail in Chapter 11.

Burden and standard of proof

Even when patients are subject to orders from the Courts (e.g. a hospital order under s.37 MHA), appeals against detention are civil (not criminal) matters. Therefore, on any issues where there is disagreement between the patient and the professionals, the Tribunal will apply what is known as the civil 'standard of proof'; they will make findings on 'the balance of probabilities', meaning whether something is more likely than not. To use a common example, is it more likely than not that a patient will continue to accept medication if they are no longer detained? This is a less strict standard of proof than that used in criminal proceedings where issues must be 'beyond reasonable doubt' and a jury must be 'sure' of a defendant's guilt.

Inquisitorial v adversarial

Tribunal proceedings in mental health cases are generally described as 'inquisitorial' rather than 'adversarial' (such as criminal cases). This means that the Tribunal can take a more proactive role in seeking evidence, questioning the patient and the professionals and taking a flexible approach to managing the case rather than solely deciding the legal issues between the patient and the detaining authority. In an adversarial criminal case the Judge's role would be more of an adjudicator in ensuring the law and legal procedures are complied with, ruling on any legal issues that arise and instructing the jury on the relevant law.

Public or private hearings?

The Tribunal Rules require that hearings be held in private unless it is in the interests of justice or the patient for the hearing to be held in public (Rule 38(1) (E), Rule 25(1) (W)).

Bartlett and Sandland (2007, p532) explain:

> *Tribunal hearings trade in confidential medical and other information about patients but also sometimes in matters that attract a public interest. Information that discloses the evidential base on which a Tribunal reached its decision, or information about any conditions imposed on discharge must remain private. This is understandable, but has the unfortunate consequence that media reports cannot include the reason for a discharge decision, which risks adding to public misunderstanding of the work of the Tribunal system.*

A public hearing is a right under Article 6 ECHR, but this obviously needs to be applied with caution and sensitivity in mental health cases and most hearings are in private. There have been some successful applications for public hearings.

The significance of the ECHR and Human Rights Act 1998

At the time of writing, the UK remains a signatory to the ECHR with rights under the Convention being incorporated in UK law by the Human Rights Act 1998 (HRA). For patients subject to the MHA, the operation of the ECHR and HRA are significant in several ways:

- First, if all appeals within the UK Court system have been exhausted, it may be open to the patient to take the case to the European Court of Human Rights where there is a claim that their rights under the Convention have been violated.

- Second, Tribunals are required, where possible, to interpret all legislation in a way that is compatible (does not conflict) with the ECHR. If this is not possible, a higher Court may make a 'declaration of incompatibility', which effectively puts the issue back to Parliament to decide whether to amend the law. This happened in 2001 when the MHA was amended to place the responsibility (known as the 'burden of proof') in most cases on the Responsible Authority (the hospital) to positively satisfy the Tribunal that the grounds for detention are still met. Before the amendment it was for the patient to satisfy the Tribunal that the grounds were no longer met (Mental Health Act 1983 (Remedial Order) Order 2001).

- Third, as is the case for all mental health professionals, Tribunals are public authorities under the HRA and therefore obliged to act consistently with the Convention in carrying out their functions.

For patients subject to the MHA, the key rights under the ECHR are:

Article 5 – Right to liberty and security

While the detention of persons of 'unsound mind' is permissible under the ECHR, this must be done by a procedure prescribed by law and, crucially, the detained person is entitled to take proceedings for the lawfulness of the detention to be decided speedily by a Court.

Article 6 – Right to fair trial

The right to a fair and public hearing within a reasonable time by an independent and impartial Tribunal established by law.

Article 8 – Right to respect for private and family life

Any interference with this right must be in accordance with the law and necessary for a number of limited reasons, the most relevant being public safety, protection of health and protection of the rights and freedoms of others. While patients in the community under a CTO or Guardianship, for example, are not 'detained' for the purposes of Article 5 ECHR, the conditions or requirements attached to these orders may amount to a significant interference with their private and family life and the legal framework provides for access to the Tribunal which is:

> *equivalent to the rights enjoyed by a patient detained in hospital so that there is no incoherence or lack of equivalence in the safeguards provided by the scheme.*

> *(SSJ v MM [2017])*

Access to the Tribunal for a patient satisfies the right to have the lawfulness of their detention decided by a Court; the right to a fair hearing by an independent and impartial Tribunal and, particularly for CTO and Guardianship patients, the lawfulness of any Article 8 interference to be challenged.

Legal Aid and representation

Patients' rights are further supported by non-means-tested Legal Aid being available for legal advice and representation in Tribunal proceedings. Legal Aid may also be available for other assistance for patients, such as representation at Hospital Managers reviews, but this is means-tested. For Legal Aid to be payable, the representative must be an accredited member of the Law Society's Mental Health Panel.

Other means for challenging detention or restrictions on liberty

This book is focused entirely on Tribunal proceedings but, for completeness, it is worth mentioning that there are other avenues for a patient to challenge their detention or restrictions on their liberty through the Courts:

Habeas corpus

First, if the patient claims that their detention is simply unlawful from the outset because of a fundamental procedural flaw they may apply to the High Court for a writ of 'habeas corpus'. A fundamental procedural flaw might be a failure to consult with a Nearest Relative (NR) or the professionals completing the section papers not being appropriately qualified. The Court will require the detaining hospital to show legal justification for the detention and if the hospital cannot do this, then the writ will be issued and the patient released.

Judicial review

Even if there is no obvious fundamental legal error, it may be open to the patient to pursue an application to the Upper Tribunal (or in some cases the High Court) for judicial review of, for example, the decision to detain or decisions concerning treatment or the level of restriction being imposed on the patient where the patient argues that the decision made is illegal, irrational or procedurally improper. The Court has a range of powers available, most importantly that the decision can be 'quashed', essentially forcing the relevant authorities to think again.

Statistics

Tribunal statistics for England can be found at data.justice.gov.uk and are usually included in the Care Quality Commission's annual Monitoring the Mental Health Act Report. Welsh Tribunal statistics are published within MHRT for Wales annual reports.

Reviewing data from 2013 to 2019 reveals a discharge rate of approximately 10–12% for detained patients and around 5% for CTO patients. The highest discharge rate is for restricted patients. This is probably because the RC does not have the power to discharge restricted patients and the only other possibility, other than the Tribunal, would be discharge by the Secretary of State (a relatively rare occurrence). A successful application by a restricted patient would usually follow a great deal of planning and many patients will apply at a time when their clinical team are in support of conditional discharge following a probably fairly lengthy period in hospital.

Many applications do not progress to a hearing because the patient withdraws their application or they are discharged by their RC (e.g. in England in 2016/2017 out of 30,079 applications, a total of 8,751 patients were discharged by their RC before the hearing (CQC, 2018)).

Hospital Managers reviews

FAQ: What is the difference between a Hospital Managers review and the Tribunal?

Answer: Hospital Managers have a range of duties under the MHA and have the power to discharge some patients. That power lies in s.23 MHA and any further guidance on how they should review the case is provided within the MHA English and Welsh Codes of Practice. This power to discharge (or not) must be carried out by non-executives and non-employees of the hospital (s.23(6)), which provides at least some element of independence.

They are not part of the judicial system but the Courts have certainly viewed Hospital Managers Panels as having the same status as Tribunals when considering whether to exercise their power under s.23 (South Staffordshire and Shropshire Healthcare NHS Foundation Trust v The Hospital Managers of St George's Hospital [2016]).

Both the English and Welsh MHA Codes of Practice oblige Hospital Managers to carry out reviews of a patient's case when a section is renewed or extended and also state that reviews should be undertaken when a patient requests it or when an NR is 'barred' from discharging a patient. In practice these functions are carried out by Panels of three non-executive 'Hospital Managers' and a well-run review might look similar to a Tribunal hearing to the casual observer.

Local authorities also have a similar power to discharge patients subject to Guardianship orders under s.7 or s.37 MHA. Section 23 also provides powers for the RC or NR to discharge most unrestricted patients.

The English and Welsh MHA Codes of Practice offer guidance to Hospital Managers on when to hold reviews and what to consider. As part of this, they rely on professionals to provide up-to-date information (orally and in writing) to assist them in deciding whether to exercise their discharge power. The guidance suggests that reports to the Hospital Managers might follow the relevant headings required by the Tribunal. Most of the guidance in this book could usefully be applied when preparing reports or providing oral evidence to a Hospital Managers' review.

Top tips

- *Keeping the status of the Tribunal in mind is probably the most important advice that could be offered to someone approaching a Tribunal hearing for the first time.*

- *Tribunal report headings set out in the Practice Direction could usefully be applied when writing reports for a Hospital Managers' review.*

Chapter summary

- Any informality at the Tribunal is for the benefit of the patient.

- The Tribunal meets the requirements of the ECHR and HRA 1998 to have speedy access to a hearing when detained or subject to compulsion in the community.

- Tribunals can discharge most patients subject to the MHA.

- Legal Aid is available to patients for legal representation in Tribunal proceedings.

- Tribunals are 'inquisitorial' and decisions are made on the 'balance of probabilities'.

- Hospital Managers (sometimes referred to as Associate Hospital Managers) Panels are not Courts. However, they have the power to discharge under s.23 MHA.

Chapter 2
Applications and references to the Tribunal

Introduction

This chapter will explain who can make applications to the Tribunal and when. It also deals with automatic references to the Tribunal.

The chapter deals initially with 'civil patients': patients under Part II MHA; for example, patients detained under s.2 or s.3 or patients subject to Guardianship or Community Treatment Orders (CTOs). The rules for patients subject to Part III MHA (patients concerned in criminal proceedings or under sentence) are different and discussed separately.

As we saw in Chapter 1, the procedural safeguards in Article 5(4) European Convention on Human Rights (ECHR) provide for a patient to *'take proceedings by which the lawfulness of his detention shall be decided speedily by a Court and his release ordered if the detention is not lawful'*. In mental health cases, this safeguard is provided by access to the Tribunal.

Case-law from the European Court of Human Rights (ECtHR) has further refined this right and established the following principles:

- A patient is entitled to initial access to a Court to challenge their detention and to take further proceedings at reasonable intervals.

- The Court must have the power to release the patient.

- Special additional safeguards and legal assistance are required to protect a person whose capacity to act for themselves may be impaired by mental disorder.

- The patient's right to access a review of their detention is in addition to any automatic reviews.

- The 'burden' is on the detaining authority to prove the lawfulness of the detention.

Applications and references

The rights of patients to apply to the Tribunal and the duties of Hospital Managers and the Secretary of State to refer cases to the Tribunal in certain circumstances are found in Part V MHA 1983 and are summarised in Table 2.1 with a more detailed explanation to follow.

Table 2.1   Applications and references grid

	When can the patient apply?	When must a statutory reference be made?
Section 2	In first 14 days	n/a
Section 3	In first six months and after any renewal	After six months from the initial date of detention (which includes any initial period of detention under s.2) if there has been no Tribunal hearing and after any three-year interval without a hearing (one-year intervals if patient is under 18)
Section 7 (Guardianship)	In first six months and after any renewal	There are no statutory references for Guardianship patients
Section 17A community treatment order (CTO)	In first six months and after any extension	After six months (if there has been no Tribunal hearing) and after any three-year interval without a hearing (one-year intervals if patient is under 18). After any CTO revocation. Note that the six-month period runs from the date of the initial detention that led to the CTO
Section 37 Hospital Order	In second six months and after any renewal	After any three-year interval without a hearing (1 year intervals if patient is under 18)
Section 37 Guardianship Order	In first six months and after any renewal	n/a
Section 37/41	In second six months and thereafter annually	After any three-year interval without a hearing
Section 45A	In second six months and thereafter annually	After any three-year interval without a hearing
S.37/41 (Conditionally Discharged)	After 12 months and then in each two-year period	n/a (although if the patient is recalled to hospital the Secretary of State must refer the case to the Tribunal within one month)
s.47 or 47/49	In first six months, second six months and thereafter annually	After any three-year interval without a hearing (1 year intervals if patient is not restricted and is under 18)
s.48 or 48/49	In first six months, second six months and thereafter annually	After any three-year interval without a hearing (1 year intervals if patient is not restricted and is under 18)

The Tribunal system provides for patients to apply for a review of their detention or community compulsion as well as a system of periodic automatic reviews. Tribunal hearings take place in four circumstances:

- A patient's application (sometimes incorrectly referred to as an appeal);

- A statutory reference to the Tribunal by the Hospital Managers or the Secretary of State or the Welsh Ministers;

- Discretionary references by the Secretary of State or the Welsh Ministers;
- Applications by the Nearest Relative (NR).

Patient applications and timescales: When and how often can a patient apply to the Tribunal?

The Reference Guide to the Mental Health Act 1983 has useful information on applications and references in Chapter 6. The MHRTW has produced a very helpful summary grid of Tribunal eligibility, which can be accessed here:

https://mentalhealthreviewTribunal.gov.wales/sites/mentalhealthreview/files/2019-05/mhrtw-17-eligibility-table-en.pdf

In summary the general principles on applications and timescales are as follows:

- The statutory rights of patients to apply to the Tribunal are found in s.66 MHA.
- For section 2 cases, the patient can apply once and the application must be made within the first 14 days of the section. There are no time limits for applications under any other section.
- A patient can apply to the Tribunal in each 'eligibility period', meaning that each time a section is renewed or a CTO is extended, the patient acquires another opportunity to apply.
- If a patient's legal status changes, for example, from a s.3 to a CTO, they acquire another right to apply.
- If a patient's legal status changes after they have applied to the Tribunal, but before the case is heard the hearing will go ahead and the Tribunal will consider the legal criteria of the new section.
- For example, if a patient applies to the Tribunal while detained under section 2 and an application for detention under section 3 is completed before the hearing, the Tribunal will hear the case and consider the section 3 criteria. This does not affect the patient's new right to appeal against the section 3, so there may be two Tribunal hearings in one period of detention.
- A patient's right to make an application is unaffected by any statutory references to the Tribunal. A patient could make their own application immediately after a statutory reference hearing which is another reason you may encounter a number of hearings in a relatively short space of time.

Hospital Managers duties to provide information

Hospital Managers have a statutory duty under s.132 and s.132A MHA to provide detained patients and patients subject to a CTO with information about their right to apply to the Tribunal. These duties extend to the provision of information to the NR where practicable unless the patient requests otherwise. There is a comparable duty on Local Authorities to ensure Guardianship patients and their NRs are given information about their rights (Reg 26.

Mental Health (Hospital) (England) Regulations 2008/Reg 15. Mental Health (Hospital, Guardianship, Community Treatment and Consent to Treatment) (Wales) Regulations 2008).

This duty is especially important for s.2 patients given the 14-day time limit for submitting an application. The application can be completed by the patient, but the form permits a person authorised by the patient to submit the application and, in practice, the form might be completed by the patient's legal representative, MHA Administrators, IMHAs or nursing staff. Both the Department of Health and Welsh Assembly have produced information leaflets covering the right to apply to the Tribunal, which should be freely available and accessible to patients. These are available on their archived website at www.webarchive.natonalarchives.gov.uk.

The Welsh Assembly leaflets are on their website at www.wales.nhs.uk and searching for 'Booklets and Leaflets'. The Mental Health Law Online website has links to both at www.mentalhealthlaw.co.uk.

Patients detained under s.3 or subject to a CTO or Guardianship can apply to the Tribunal at any stage during the initial six months, and again each time the sections are renewed or extended.

The Tribunal will notify the hospital and the patient (or their representative if they have one), that an application or reference has been received.

Information to patients on how to access representation should be easily accessible and available. Non-means-tested Legal Aid is available for representation at Tribunals, and this should be made clear to patients to avoid situations where the patient does not seek legal advice because they fear this will be costly to them.

Statutory references by Hospital Managers

The reference system provides an additional safeguard for patients who, for whatever reason, do not apply to the Tribunal. This could be due to capacity issues, degree of illness, passivity, a lack of belief in the merits of an appeal or anxieties about embarking on a legal procedure. The reference system provides for automatic periodic reviews of a patient's detention or community compulsion by the Tribunal whether the patient wants this or not. The duties on Hospital Managers to refer cases to the Tribunal can be found in s.68 MHA (summarised above in Table 2.1) and the duty is triggered in the following circumstances:

- When six months has elapsed since the patient was first detained if there has been no Tribunal application or reference in that period. Note that the six-month period runs from the first day of detention so, if a patient is detained under s.2, then s.3 and then discharged under a CTO, the six months runs from the start of the s.2.

- When a patient's CTO is revoked.

- After any three-year period when the patient's case has not been considered by the Tribunal.

- For under 18s, after any one-year period when the patient's case has not been considered by the Tribunal.

The duty of Hospital Managers includes unrestricted Part III patients (e.g. patients subject to s.37 hospital orders) whose cases must be referred after any three-year interval without a hearing taking place (1 year intervals for under 18s).

Once an application or reference is received, the Tribunal procedure is exactly the same. The required application, reference and other forms for the Tribunals can be found at:

www.gov.uk/government/collections/mental-health-Tribunal-forms (England)

https://mentalhealthreviewTribunal.gov.wales/guidance-and-forms (Wales)

Discretionary references by the Secretary of State or Welsh Ministers

The Secretary of State and Welsh Ministers have a general discretion under s.67 MHA to refer a Part II patient's case to the Tribunal at any time – even if the patient is not eligible to apply themselves. Anyone can request a reference and requests are made to the Department of Health and Social Care or Welsh Assembly.

The request for a discretionary reference must provide supporting evidence explaining the reasons for the request; when the Tribunal last considered the case and when the patient will next be eligible to apply or a statutory reference will be due. The Department of Health and Social Care has issued guidance to assist with such requests (s.67 MHA 1983: References by the Secretary of State for Health and Social Care to the First-tier Tribunal. August 2019).

FAQ: When is it most likely that a reference to the Tribunal is requested and why?

Answer: A reference could be requested when a s.2 patient has failed to apply to the Tribunal within the 14-day time limit perhaps because of their mental state, capacity issues or due to lack of adequate information being provided to them. A reference could also be requested if a s.2 has been extended while an application to displace an NR is being considered by the County Court.

The MHA Codes of Practice (Para 37.45–37.46 (E), 37.40 (W)) also advise Hospital Managers to consider asking the Secretary of State to refer patients where there is a general concern that the patient's Article 5 rights 'might otherwise be at risk of being violated because they are unable (for whatever reason) to have their cases considered by the Tribunal speedily following their initial detention or at reasonable intervals afterwards'. A patient lacking capacity to apply to the Tribunal would be the obvious example.

Capacity issues?

Case-law has found the reference system to provide adequate protection of Article 5 ECHR rights for patients lacking the capacity to pursue their own application to the Tribunal. However, the European Court of Human Rights (ECtHR) has found the limited access to the Tribunal for incapacitated patients detained under s.2 to be an Article 5 violation. See the case example below.

ACTIVITY *2.1*

Read the case example below. How might you assist a patient such as MH to access a review of their detention?

CASE EXAMPLE

MH v UK *[2013] ECHR 1008*

MH was a woman with severe disabilities as a result of Downs Syndrome who resided with her Mother (her NR). She was removed from her home and detained under s.2 MHA. She did not apply to the Tribunal within the first 14 days of her detention and lacked the legal capacity to do so. Her Mother ordered her discharge and was 'barred' by the Responsible Clinician (RC). Her Mother had no right to apply to the Tribunal herself. An application was made to the County Court to displace her Mother as NR. The section 2 was extended beyond the usual 28-day period while these proceedings were being decided. Mother instructed solicitors who requested a discretionary reference to the Tribunal by the Secretary of State. The reference was made and a Tribunal hearing took place nearly two months after MH's detention. The Tribunal did not discharge the s.2. MH was eventually discharged to residential accommodation after a total of six months' detention.

After a complex legal pathway, the case came before the ECtHR, who found that MH's Article 5 ECHR rights had been breached because of her inability to access the Tribunal. The actions of her Mother, her Mother's solicitors and the Secretary of State, which led to the discretionary reference to the Tribunal were insufficient as this relied on goodwill and discretion. Special safeguards were required for patients lacking legal competence.

The UK Government's response to this case was to point to the provision of IMHAs since the MHA 2007. While it is true that an IMHA can advise a patient of their rights and even contact a lawyer on the patient's behalf, subsequent case-law has found that incapacity to apply to the Tribunal may also mean an incapacity to authorise another person to apply on their behalf and therefore such applications are likely to be struck out (i.e. deemed invalid). It also remains the case that, for ethical reasons, a mental health lawyer could not act for a client lacking the capacity to instruct them unless appointed by the Tribunal, and therefore we suggest the Government's reliance on the availability of IMHAs to be an unsatisfactory response to the issues raised in the case.

The question of the patient's capacity in relation to Tribunal proceedings has become complex and has generated a large amount of case-law. Not least because there are different issues that arise when considering the capacity to apply to the Tribunal; capacity to appoint a legal representative; capacity to provide instructions to a representative; and capacity to litigate (to conduct the proceedings). Although the test for capacity is within the Mental Capacity Act 2005 (MCA), the level of understanding required is different for each of these decisions.

The test for capacity to apply to the Tribunal has been set by the Upper Tribunal at a fairly low level, and a patient simply needs to understand that they are being detained against their will and that the Tribunal can decide on whether they should be released (*VS v St. Andrew's Healthcare* [2018]). See Chapter 8 for a more detailed discussion of capacity issues.

Applications by Nearest Relatives

The NR has a number of important rights and powers in respect of detained patients and patients subject to compulsion in the community: an NR may object to an application for admission under s.3 or to a Guardianship application under s.7 and an NR may, under s.23 MHA, order the discharge of patients subject to s.2, s.3, s.7 Guardianship and s.17A CTOs. This might be 'barred' by the RC under s.25 (except in Guardianship cases where the RC has no power to bar an order for discharge by the NR) but in certain circumstances (s.3 and CTO cases), this would then allow the NR to apply to the Tribunal. Also, if the NR is set aside (displaced) under s.29 by the County Court, they still retain a right to apply to the Tribunal in every 12-month period that the order is in place (s.66 (2)(g)).

Table 2.2   Nearest Relative Tribunal applications summary grid

	NR right to object	NR right to order discharge	RC power to bar an NR discharge order	NR right to apply to the Tribunal
s.2	No	Yes	Yes	No
s.3	Yes	Yes	Yes	Yes – if barred by RC
s.7 (Guardianship)	Yes	Yes	No	No
s.17A (CTO)	No	Yes	Yes	Yes – if barred by RC

From Table 2.2 we can see that an NR can only apply to the Tribunal when they have exercised their power to order discharge of a patient detained under s.3 or subject to a CTO and the order for discharge has then been barred by the RC under s.25. For Guardianship patients, an NR order for discharge cannot be barred; therefore, there is no need for access to the Tribunal. NRs also acquire a right to apply to the Tribunal when they are 'displaced' by the County Court as Nearest Relative on certain grounds (s.66(1)(h)).

For s.2 patients, the NR has no access to the Tribunal in any circumstances (although they could request a discretionary reference by the Secretary of State). Because of the limited period of detention under s.2 (up to 28 days) and the patient's own right to apply to the Tribunal, the Courts have found the lack of any NR power to apply does not breach any Article 5 ECHR rights (*MA v SSH* [2012]).

The position for NRs of Part III patients is different and considered separately below.

Part III patients

> **FAQ: Why is access to the Tribunal more limited for Part III patients?**
>
> *Answer: The general rule is that where the detention is as a result of a Court order, the case has been considered by a Court at the outset and therefore the right to seek a review of the detention by a Court is delayed for six months.*

So, patients detained under s.37, s.37/41 or s.45A can apply to the Tribunal six months *after* the date of the order. This rule does not apply to patients who have been transferred from prison under s.47 or s.48 because such transfers are not ordered by a Court (they are authorised by transfer warrants issued by the Secretary of State) so transferred patients can apply to the Tribunal immediately. The other exception is that patients subject to Guardianship orders under s.37 can also apply within the first six months.

Otherwise, the position for Part III patients is no different and a further Tribunal application can be made each time a s.37 hospital order or Guardianship order is renewed. Restriction orders are indefinite and not renewed as such, but patients subject to restriction orders (including restriction directions or limitation directions) may apply once in the second six months and then once in each year of detention. You may hear the term 'eligibility periods', which simply means each period of time that an application could be made.

Patients subject to shorter-term powers under Part III (remands to hospital under s.35 or s.36 or interim hospital orders under s.38) have no rights to apply to the Tribunal because a final sentencing decision has not been made by the criminal Courts.

For Part III patients the role of the NR is much more limited and restricted patients are treated as having no NR at all. NRs of patients subject to unrestricted hospital orders under s.37 may apply to the Tribunal whenever the patient would be eligible – i.e. the second six months and then annually. NRs of patients subject to Guardianship orders under s.37 can apply in the first 12 months and then annually.

The Tribunal's powers in respect of both unrestricted and restricted patients are considered in detail in Chapter 3.

Part III restricted patients – references

The duties to refer restricted patients to the Tribunal in some circumstances rest with the Secretary of State (s.71) rather than with the Hospital Managers. This duty sits alongside the extensive role that the Secretary of State has in respect of restricted patients: to make decisions about matters such as leave or transfer, for example. The duties and powers of the

Secretary of State include patients in Wales as they have not been devolved to the Welsh Ministers. The duties can be summarised as follows:

- A reference must be made after any three-year interval where no hearing has taken place (this includes under 18s).

- The Secretary of State also has a general discretion to refer a case at any time (s.71(1)).

- If a conditionally discharged patient is recalled to hospital then the Secretary of State must refer the case to the Tribunal within one month of the patient's return to hospital (s.75(1)(a)).

ACTIVITY 2.2

Mr B has been detained on s.2 and then on s.3.

Following four months of detention on the s.3 he is then discharged on to a CTO.

He has not appealed against his CTO and this has recently been extended for a further six months.

Questions:

- *At which points could Mr B apply to the Tribunal?*

- *At what points must the Hospital Managers refer his case to the Tribunal if he has not applied?*

Questions:

- *In what situations might his NR be able to apply in their own right to the Tribunal?*

Top tips

- *Patients should be offered a list of Law Society accredited legal representatives by the Hospital Managers.*

- *'Rights' leaflets should be freely available to patients, and they should also be informed of their right to an IMHA.*

- *For patients lacking the capacity to make their own application, consideration should be given to whether seeking a discretionary reference to the Tribunal by the Secretary of State is appropriate.*

Chapter summary

- The MHA provides for patients to be able to apply to the Tribunal at regular intervals during a period of detention or community compulsion.

- The system of references to the Tribunal provides further safeguards for patients who, for whatever reason, do not or cannot exercise their own rights to apply.

- Nearest Relatives can also apply to the Tribunal in certain circumstances.

- The right to have a case heard by the Tribunal ensures compliance with the patient's Article 5 ECHR rights.

Chapter 3

What powers and duties does the Tribunal have?

Introduction

In this chapter we shall look at the key powers and duties of the Tribunal: both the statutory power, and in some circumstances a duty, to order discharge and make statutory recommendations and the 'softer' non-statutory powers to make informal recommendations or to use case management powers to progress the patient's case.

FAQ: What is meant by a legal power or duty?

Answer: Statutory powers are often described as a 'can do'. They are set out in law but are discretionary.

A statutory duty is often described as a 'must or shall do', which must be applied if the law dictates.

For example, s.72 Mental Health Act (MHA) states that the Tribunal 'shall direct the discharge' of a patient (in certain specified circumstances, which we shall look at in detail below).

As we saw in Chapter 1, compliance with Article 5 European Convention on Human Rights (ECHR) requires not just the right for the patient to bring proceedings to challenge the lawfulness of detention, but the judicial body hearing such a case *must* have the power to release the patient. In most Tribunal proceedings it is likely that the patient will be seeking discharge from detention or community compulsion.

This chapter will focus initially on unrestricted detained patients, as these are the cases that professionals will most frequently be dealing with. The Tribunal's powers in respect of Community Treatment Order (CTO), Guardianship and restricted patients are slightly different and more limited in some cases and these are dealt with separately at the end of the chapter.

Unrestricted detained patients (s.2, s.3, s.37, s.47, s.48)

Discharge

The powers of Tribunals in respect of these patients are governed by s.72 MHA. The specific legal grounds that Tribunals must apply are considered in more detail in Chapter 6; however, in general terms, the Tribunal will consider whether the patient is suffering from any mental disorder; if so, whether the disorder is of a nature or a degree to warrant or make continued detention appropriate and whether detention remains justified or necessary in the interests of the patient's health, their safety or for the protection of others.

With the exception of s.2 cases, the Tribunal must also consider whether appropriate medical treatment is available (s.72(1)(b)(iia)). This language is likely to be familiar to professionals as the criteria applied by the Tribunal largely mirror the grounds for admission under the MHA.

If the Tribunal is not satisfied that any of the criteria continue to be met it is under a duty to discharge the patient from detention. The 'burden' in most cases is on the Responsible Authority (i.e. the hospital cases) to positively satisfy the Tribunal that the grounds for detention continue to be met. This means that there will be particular scrutiny of professional evidence that is supporting continued detention. There is no onus on a detained patient to satisfy the Tribunal of anything.

The Tribunal also has a (very rarely used) general discretion to discharge a patient even if the statutory criteria are met (s.72(1)). This would only be exercised in exceptional circumstances where, perhaps, it is felt that despite the criteria being met, treatment and care can be provided in an alternative setting. Jones (2020) cites the example of a patient being granted a discretionary discharge in order to travel overseas to re-join family and to receive treatment there. We have also encountered this power being exercised in respect of very young children where Tribunals have considered that, despite the legal criteria for detention being met, a combination of family support and community support from children's services and mental health services made it more appropriate for the patient to be cared for at home.

Discharge on a future date (s.72(3))

Commonly described as delayed or deferred discharge. As it sounds, this is the power to direct that the patient be discharged from detention at a later date. This means that the Tribunal is not satisfied that the grounds for continued detention are met and is exercising its duty to discharge but for pragmatic reasons feel that a delay in the discharge taking effect is required. It is almost always employed to allow services time to put the necessary support and treatment arrangements in place in the community. In advance of the hearing, professionals should have considered the possibility and planned for a Tribunal decision to discharge, and you will see in the section titled 'social circumstances reports' at the end of Chapter 7 that the Practice Direction on reports requires social circumstances reports (SCRs) for inpatients to set out *'the details of any Care Pathway* [sic] *Approach (CPA) and/ or Section 117 aftercare plan in full or in embryo …'*.

A Tribunal has met to hear the case of John, currently detained under s.3 MHA.

The Tribunal is minded to discharge John from the section as the statutory criteria are no longer fulfilled.

However, it is Friday afternoon and the Care Coordinator informs the Tribunal that services would have little or no time to put in place a robust follow-up ahead of the weekend. They would require referral to the home treatment team, and the community team needs to ensure that John's flat is ready for him to return to as there have been some problems there.

The professionals are agreed that discharging John at the start of the weekend is likely to leave him without the required support and therefore at increased risk.

Question:

* *Does the Tribunal need to discharge John immediately given that he does not meet the criteria? What other powers might they have?*

Our experience has been that a brief deferral is particularly likely when the Tribunal hearing falls on a Friday afternoon when services would have little or no time for the team to put services in place before the weekend. A direction for discharge at a later date cannot be reversed and therefore the Courts have held that this power cannot be used for 'testing out' whether the patient is ready for discharge (*CNWL NHS Foundation Trust v H-JH* [2012]) and that, if there is any uncertainty as to the form or availability of community support, the appropriate course of action would be to adjourn rather than make such a direction (*R(H) v Ashworth Hospital Authority* [2002]). A Tribunal is likely to require clear evidence that services will be in place before the discharge takes effect before using this power.

Statutory recommendations (s.72(3) and (3A))

Even if the patient is deemed to be in need of continued detention, the Tribunal has the power to make the following statutory recommendations for the sole purpose of facilitating discharge at a later date:

* Section 17 leave;
* Transfer to another hospital;
* Transfer into Guardianship.

The Tribunal can also make a statutory recommendation:

* That the Responsible Clinician (RC) consider whether to make a Community Treatment Order (CTO).

A recommendation does not compel the detaining authority to take any steps; however, if the recommendation is not complied with, it is open to the Tribunal to reconvene and reconsider the case afresh, which may place a certain amount of pressure on professionals to cooperate. Generally, Tribunals will not make any statutory recommendation where it is clear that the matter is being considered or kept under review by professionals, as a recommendation will have no practical value (*RB v Nottinghamshire Healthcare NHS Trust* [2011]).

FAQ: Why does a patient apply to the Tribunal when it would appear to professionals that they have little or no prospect of being discharged? Or that discharge might be risky to them or others?

Answer: The patient has a right to a hearing as we saw in Chapter 1.

A legal representative might advise the patient that although their chances of discharge might be limited, there are a range of other things the Tribunal could do with a view to discharge at a later date or generally progressing the patient's case. See below for some examples.

Securing a statutory recommendation might be the motivating factor for the patient in these cases: securing s.17 leave can be essential to progress towards discharge, and transfer may be important to the patient if they are detained out of the area and away from family and friends or seeking to step-down to a less secure setting. Proximity to family would not, in itself, be sufficient for a recommendation to be made, but it can often be argued that being closer to local support networks would indeed facilitate discharge on a later date. If the patient is expressing a willingness to cooperate with treatment and support in the community, then they might wish to seek a recommendation that a CTO be considered or for transfer in to Guardianship as an alternative to being discharged from detention entirely or at least to try and speed up discharge/s.117 planning.

Professionals may see legal representatives presenting something of a shopping list to the Tribunal, i.e. seeking discharge or a recommendation for transfer or a recommendation for leave, etc. As discharge from detention by Tribunals is relatively infrequent then this approach might be taken in order to secure some sort of positive outcome for the patient.

Informal recommendations

The Tribunal's statutory powers are limited to the matters discussed above, and the Courts have repeatedly held that the Tribunal has no power to do anything unless permitted by the statute (s.72 MHA in this case), and we have seen that the Tribunal has no jurisdiction over treatment or the conditions of detention.

However, a Tribunal might be willing to make an informal recommendation or a narrative comment in their written decision to assist a patient. Examples would be to suggest particular assessments, investigations or activities; to encourage contact with family members or to suggest that s.117 planning should commence at an early stage. These comments are of no legal force but might be of some persuasive use.

Case management powers

The Tribunal Procedure Rules provide the Tribunal with a wide range of case management powers that might be used to progress the patient's case. The overriding objective of the Rules is to deal with the case fairly and justly and in pursuit of this objective, the Rules empower the Tribunal to, amongst other things:

- Require particular documents to be filed;
- Adjourn or postpone a hearing;
- Appoint a legal representative for the patient;
- Order disclosure of information to the patient or their legal representative;
- Summon a witness to attend the hearing to give evidence.

These case management powers may be exercised by the Tribunal Office before a hearing or by a Tribunal Panel during a hearing or following an adjourned hearing. The Tribunal might consider using these powers if it took the view that it might be in a position to discharge or make a statutory recommendation if adequate arrangements were in place and there has been significant delay in these arrangements being made. For example, when there is an undue delay in securing appropriate accommodation and this is materially preventing progress towards discharge. In practice, these sorts of directions can be very effective in progressing the patient's case towards discharge from detention. Tribunals have been known to summon very senior staff such as Chief Executives of NHS Trusts or Directors of Social Services in particularly difficult cases.

The case vignette below is a good example of how a Tribunal might use their powers to expedite discharge for the patient.

CASE STUDY

Mr A

Mr A is detained at Camberwick Green Hospital some 150 miles from his home town of Chigley. A Tribunal convenes to hear his application for discharge from detention under s.3. No representative from his local mental health service attends the hearing and no report detailing local facilities has been provided. The RC says that Mr A has made excellent progress and he would be considering a CTO if he could be confident that robust follow-up would be in place and, crucially, that Mr A has appropriate supported accommodation. The Tribunal adjourns the hearing and makes directions that the local service provide a proper social circumstances report and that a representative attends the rearranged hearing. The Tribunal reconvenes six weeks later and a social worker from the local service attends having provided a detailed report. The Tribunal hears that there are a number of suitable

(Continued)

supported housing schemes but that the case is on some sort of waiting list to be heard by the local funding Panel. The medical evidence remains positive. The Tribunal takes the view that Mr A is now being treated in unnecessarily restrictive conditions. They adjourn again and now direct that the Chair of the funding Panel attend the next hearing to explain the delay. Funding is agreed within a few weeks of this decision; Mr A begins some trial s.17 leave at a local hostel which goes very well, to the extent that the RC no longer considers a CTO to be required and Mr A is discharged.

As we can see from the scenario above, the Tribunal can use its powers in order to push things along in situations where progress has stagnated. In particular where the patient is in a more restrictive setting than is now required, but services are not being sufficiently proactive in moving the patient on.

CTO and Guardianship patients

These cases are also governed by s.72 MHA, and most of the points above apply save that the criteria for discharge are slightly different and the powers to make statutory recommendations to facilitate discharge on a future date do not apply (because the patient is already out of hospital). It is also worth noting again that, in Guardianship cases, the burden remains on the patient to demonstrate that the legal criteria are not met. As we have seen, when the MHA was amended in 2001 the burden was placed on the detaining authority to positively satisfy the Tribunal that the criteria continue to be met in most cases.

The Tribunal has no powers in respect of the specific conditions attached to a CTO and cannot vary, remove or add to the conditions, although a Tribunal could make an informal comment in their decision if it were felt that, for example, a particular condition was unnecessary, redundant or disproportionate. This is a curious contrast with conditionally discharged restricted patients where the Tribunal can add, vary or remove conditions – one might have expected that there would be less control over the conditions for restricted patients.

Restricted patients (s.37/41)

The Tribunal's powers in respect of restricted patients are found in s.73 MHA. Restricted patients can also be discharged by the Secretary of State (s.42), although this is relatively rare. RCs and Hospital Managers effectively have no power to discharge restricted patients because the consent of the Secretary of State is required. The Tribunal has no general discretion to discharge restricted patients; however, they are under a duty to discharge if not satisfied that the statutory criteria are met.

Absolute discharge

As it sounds, this is the power to discharge the patient from detention in hospital without any conditions or continuing legal framework. Absolute discharges directly from hospital are rare as one might expect, given that patients subject to s.37/41 are detained as a result of a criminal offence and an assessment by the Court that the restriction order is necessary to protect the public from serious harm.

Conditional discharge

Conditional discharge has been described as a CTO for restricted patients (Hale, 2010, p245). Conditional discharge is the most likely pathway out of detention in hospital for restricted patients. Again, as it sounds, this is discharge subject to usually very stringent conditions, with the Secretary of State retaining the power to recall the patient to hospital. There is no legal threshold for recalling a patient; however, the MHA Codes (22.82 (E), 22.83 (W)) identify a number of factors that might indicate the need for recall: public safety being the most important along with a change in circumstances giving rise to risks which are associated with the patient's mental disorder.

There are no limits on the number or nature of the conditions that can be imposed by the Tribunal save that, as a result of the Supreme Court decision in the *'MM'* case, the conditions may not amount to a deprivation of the patient's liberty (*Secretary of State for Justice v MM* [2018]).

This has become a complex area after a number of cases concerning patients with learning disabilities presenting a risk of offending and requiring levels of supervision in the community that amount to a deprivation of liberty. For patients deemed to lack capacity to consent to such a regime, it is possible for the Tribunal proceedings to coordinate with an application to the Court of Protection or a request for a Deprivation of Liberty Safeguards (DoLS) authorisation to make any deprivation of liberty lawful (*MC v Cygnet Behavioural Health Ltd and Secretary of State for Justice* [2020]). For patients with capacity, the position remains unsatisfactorily problematic: use of long periods of s.17 leave has been suggested in guidance from the Secretary of State, and there have also been some successful applications for the use of the inherent jurisdiction of the High Court to authorise the deprivation of liberty of conditionally discharged patients (*Re AB (Inherent Jurisdiction: Deprivation of Liberty)* [2018]).

The coordination between different jurisdictions (e.g. the Tribunal and the Court of Protection) can be complex and may give rise to a number of adjournments while these arrangements are being made.

Conditions will almost always include compliance with clinical and social supervision and will always include a condition of residence at a specified address, and may also include submission to drug or alcohol testing or adhering to an exclusion zone to prevent proximity to any victims. The Secretary of State has the power to vary the conditions (s.73(5)).

A patient who has been conditionally discharged may apply to the Tribunal after 12 months (s.75). In these cases, the Tribunal's powers are limited to granting an absolute discharge or not or varying the conditions that were imposed when the patient left hospital – this could include removing all of the conditions with only the liability to recall remaining. You may find that legal representatives might often ask for absolute discharge or alternatively that the conditions are removed, as this would give the patient the opportunity to demonstrate further progress in the community without specific conditions before pursuing an absolute discharge again.

Along with Guardianship patients, these are the other cases where the 'burden' remains on the patient to satisfy the Tribunal that the conditions and recall power are no longer necessary.

Deferred direction for conditional discharge (s.73(7))

This is similar to the delayed discharge powers discussed above and is also usually employed to allow time for aftercare arrangements to be put in place. However, it cannot be to a specified date and it does not mean the patient will necessarily be discharged. To use this power, the Tribunal must be in a position to draft the conditions of discharge (if there is any doubt or uncertainty they should adjourn). If satisfied at a later date that the necessary arrangements are in place and the conditions can take effect then the Tribunal can lift the deferral and the conditional discharge will proceed. This power cannot be used to gather information or for any sort of testing out of the patient. A decision to defer a direction for conditional discharge can be reversed by a Tribunal if the necessary arrangements prove impossible to implement, for example, no psychiatrist can be found willing to take on clinical supervision responsibility in the community (*R(H) v MHRT for the Mersey Regional Health Authority* [1986]).

Extra-statutory recommendations

Unlike the position for unrestricted patients (above), the Tribunal has no power to make statutory recommendations. A practice developed of Tribunals making what became known as extra-statutory recommendations (ESRs) about matters such as s.17 leave or transfer to less secure settings. The hope being that such comment will be given some weight by the Secretary of State if a subsequent application is made by the patient's RC for leave or transfer. However, case-law has circumscribed this practice and, while a Tribunal might still be willing to make informal narrative comments or recommendations, the patient has no legitimate expectation of this and a refusal to make such a recommendation is not appealable (*C v Birmingham and Solihull Mental Health NHS Trust* [2013] EWCA Civ 701). Legal representatives will usually seek to link leave or transfer to 'appropriate treatment' when asking the Tribunal for an ESR. For example, if a representative can link stepping down to lower security and access to more therapeutic activity as an appropriate part of medical treatment the Tribunal may consider making an ESR.

Patients subject to limitation or restriction directions (s.47/49, s.48/49, s.45A)

These are the cases where the patient retains the legal status of prisoner either because they have been transferred from prison to hospital either before or after sentencing or they have been made subject to a 'hybrid order' under s.45A which means that there is a concurrent prison sentence alongside detention under the MHA.

For all of these patients the Secretary of State has the power to return the patient to prison (s.50) until the patient reaches their earliest date of release or EDR (i.e. the date they would have been eligible for release from prison). For example, a patient becomes unwell while serving a prison sentence, is transferred to hospital, is successfully treated and recovers and is then remitted back to prison.

As one might expect, the Tribunal's powers in respect of these patients are much more limited and are found in s.74 and, most importantly, they have no power to discharge the patient. The rationale being that release from detention for this group of patients, whether from hospital or prison is ultimately a matter for the Secretary of State or the Parole Board.

In these cases, the Tribunal conducts a slightly abstract exercise by approaching the case as though the patient were actually detained under s.37/41 (see above). The Tribunal can then give a notification to the Secretary of State that, if the patient were subject to s.37/41, they would be entitled to absolute or conditional discharge. If the patient is an un-sentenced prisoner, then they will always be remitted back to prison, unless the Tribunal has also recommended that the patient continues to be detained in hospital. In the other cases, the Secretary of State has the discretion to agree to discharge and also the power to remit to prison (s.50). Patients might pursue a Tribunal application because they wish to return to prison with the benefit of a definite release date.

If the Tribunal has taken the view that the patient would be entitled to discharge, then they may also recommend to the Secretary of State that, if the patient is not released, the patient should remain in hospital (rather than return to prison). A notification under s.74 will trigger a referral to the Parole Board or entitle the patient to apply to the Parole Board when they have served their minimum sentence and some patients may pursue an application with a view to continuing treatment in hospital pending the Parole Board hearing the case at the hospital and deciding on whether or not to release.

The Tribunal might make such a recommendation when there is concern that a return to prison may cause a deterioration in the patient's mental health or undermine the progress that the patient has made while in hospital or when some form of therapeutic intervention is incomplete.

Top tips

- *Professionals should consider the possibility of the patient being discharged from detention and what their plans would be in response to this happening.*

- *It is also worth considering whether the patient is being treated in an unnecessarily restrictive environment and to prepare for questions about this.*

- *Tribunals can summon professionals, even very senior professionals if, for example, the patients progress towards discharge is being delayed by administrative rather than clinical reasons.*

Chapter summary

- In most cases, the Tribunal's most important power is to order discharge from detention or community compulsion.

- In most cases, the onus is on professionals to positively satisfy the Tribunal of the need for continued detention.

- The Tribunal has a range of softer powers that could be employed to assist the patient.

- The powers in respect of restricted patients are more limited as statutory recommendations cannot be made and there is no general discretion to discharge.

- The Tribunal has no power to discharge a patient subject to a concurrent prison sentence, or prisoners who have been transferred to hospital, if the Secretary of State has imposed further restrictions under s.49.

Chapter 4

Who is on the Tribunal Panel and what are their roles?

Introduction

This chapter will explain the constitution of the Tribunal Panel and what each Panel Member's role is. We shall look in more detail at the likely questions Panel Members will ask professionals in Chapter 9. There is also an explanation of some of the other people behind the scenes or in attendance at the hearing.

Panel Members: Appointment and configuration

As we saw in Chapter 1, the English and Welsh Tribunal systems now have different statutory bases, but there is little difference in practice. In both countries, members are appointed by the Lord Chancellor, following a selection process.

The Tribunal Panel is made up of three members with specific expertise and experience, as follows:

- A Judge who will always chair proceedings. In Wales, this is referred to as presiding over proceedings;

- A Medical Member;

- A Specialist Lay Member (in Wales referred to as the Lay Member).

Tribunal Members' roles

The Legal Member (commonly referred to as the Judge, and we have used this term throughout the text) is a qualified lawyer with appropriate experience and will chair (or preside over) the Tribunal hearing. They may or may not have experience of representing patients at Tribunals. Judges are mainly fee-paid lawyers, meaning they are paid a fee for each hearing rather than sitting as a full-time job, or Judges from other jurisdictions such as the criminal Courts. There are a smaller group of salaried Judges in England who are appointed full time and have some additional senior responsibilities. Restricted cases will be heard by a salaried or more senior Judge. At the time of writing, there are no salaried Judges in Wales other than the President.

The *Medical Member* must be a registered medical practitioner (who is a Fellow, Associate or Specialist Associate of the Royal College of Psychiatry) and has held a full-time or part-time consultant psychiatry post for at least three years, one of which should normally be within the last five years. In Wales (but not in England) Medical Members are required to hold a licence to practice.

The *Specialist Lay Member* (SpLM) (England) or *Lay Member* (Wales) must have experience in administration, such knowledge of social services or such other qualifications or experience as the Lord Chancellor considers suitable. These Panel Members might be social workers, nurses, Mental Health Act Administrators, IMHAs, etc., with significant professional experience of community services and provision of aftercare.

Their title is a little confusing and, given the requirement for expertise in practice, 'it is wrong to think of them as "lay" members' (Hale, 2017, p285).

According to the Judicial Appointments Commission:

> *Specialist Lay Members have experience in a professional capacity of working with people with mental disorders either in hospital or the community. They use their experience and knowledge to advise the other Tribunal members.*
>
> *(https://judicialappointments.gov.uk/eligibility-non-legal-roles)*

It is important to note that *any* member of the Tribunal Panel may also have experience as a user of mental health services or a carer of someone in mental health services, and they may bring this expertise to their role.

Tribunal Panel Members are required to show specific competencies set by the Judicial Appointments Commission (JAC) and will be appraised against those competencies during their period of office. Usually, members must vacate office when they reach 70 years of age, although there is discretion for members to continue to sit until 75 years.

Tribunal Panels must be composed of at least three members and at least one from each of the groups above. In some limited circumstances (reference cases for CTO patients) in England, the patient can opt to have their case dealt with by the Tribunal by way of a paper review instead of a full hearing, but these still require a Panel of at least three (see Chapter 4 for more detail about paper reviews in England only).

FAQ: Why is a Tribunal hearing not just with one Judge?

Answer: This is a reflection of the highly specialised nature of the mental health jurisdiction, which involves a complex interplay of legal, medical and social matters. When appointing Tribunal Members the Lord Chancellor must have regard to:

> the need for members of Tribunals to be experts in the subject-matter of, or the law to be applied in, cases in which they decide matters.
>
> *(s.2(3)(c) Tribunal, Courts and Enforcement Act 2007)*

Role of Panel Members

We shall look in detail in Chapter 9 at the sort of questions that each Tribunal Member might ask at a hearing. Below is an overview of each member's role.

Although the Judge will write up the decision (written reasons), the decision is made by all three Panel Members on a majority. The Tribunal operates as a single decision-maker and any dissenting view within the Panel Members is not recorded in the written decision.

An appeal against a decision will be against the Tribunal as a whole and therefore all Panel Members have a responsibility to identify and communicate any concerns they might have and to bring these to the attention of their colleagues on the Panel.

For more details on how the Tribunal reach their decision please see Chapter 6.

Apart from their specific roles, detailed below, there is some flexibility in order to deal with cases fairly and justly. The overriding objective of the Tribunal includes '*using any special expertise of the Tribunal effectively*' (Rule 2(2)(d) (E), Rule 3(2)(c) (W)). So, if any member of the Panel has particular expertise in the field of learning disability, for example, it may be that they will take on an enhanced role in the questioning of the professionals and the patient and perhaps provide advice to their Panel colleagues.

In England, a Panel of members who hold specialist expertise in Children and Adolescent Mental Health (CAMHS Panel) has been developed. The purpose of this is to ensure that at least one member of a Tribunal hearing a CAMHS case has specialist expertise in the care and treatment of under 18s. This is not a legal duty, but the Tribunal will try wherever possible to ensure one member of the Panel has this expertise. At the time of writing there is no equivalent Panel in the MHRTW.

In many hearings you will find that the Judge will ask the legal questions and focus on the statutory criteria; the Medical Member will lead the questioning of the doctor, and the SpLM will lead the questioning of the author of the social circumstances report. However, Panel Members are not bound by any particular rules and can ask questions of any witness. Hence, the Medical Member might ask the author of the social circumstances report about aftercare, and the SpLM might ask the treating doctor or clinician about, for example, diagnosis, treatment, physical health issues, etc.

The Mental Health Act (MHA) Code (12.39 (E)) states:

> *The Tribunal should ensure Panel Members understand equality issues and that there are sufficient numbers of Panel Members with a specialised understanding of the specific needs of particular groups including those listed below and that Panel Members can communicate effectively with them;*

- *Patients from minority cultural or ethnic backgrounds*
- *Patients with physical impairments and/or sensory impairments, and/or*
- *Patients with learning disabilities and/or autistic spectrum disorders.*

The MHA Code for Wales has a similar expectation of Tribunal Members (Para 12.29).

Tribunal Members attend mandatory training on a range of issues, including those above.

Role of the Judge

The Judge will always chair or preside over proceedings. The Tribunal Rules allow flexibility in how the hearing will be conducted, but the Judge must ensure the hearing is conducted fairly and that any reasonable adjustments (under the Equality Act 2010) are made and that all relevant rules and procedures are followed. They are also required to draft decisions (written reasons) following the conclusion of the hearing.

They will rely on the Medical Member to offer specialist knowledge of psychiatry and on the Specialist Lay Member to offer specialist knowledge of health and social services, in particular community services on discharge.

In practice, the Judge will usually introduce the Panel and explain the process to the patient, check who is present, which reports everyone has seen and any other initial matters. They will often start proceedings by checking with the legal representative what the patient is seeking or whether there are any preliminary matters to be dealt with before the substantive hearing commences. They will usually go through the legal criteria with the Responsible Clinician (RC) to establish what grounds are being relied on by the detaining authority before handing over further questioning of the RC to the Medical Member. We shall look further at the process and questioning of witnesses in Chapter 9. Some Judges may leave much of the questioning to the other Panel Members, asking any supplementary questions at the end where something has not been covered.

Judges take contemporaneous notes during the hearing, which are then used to record the final decision and reasons. There is no stenographer and no electronic recording permitted in the Tribunal and therefore the Judge is tasked with taking a clear and accurate note of the evidence. Judges increasingly make use of laptops or tablets to take notes.

Role of the Medical Member

The Medical Member's role is to assist the Panel with information specific to psychiatry, diagnosis, treatment, prognosis and risks to the person or others as a result of any mental disorder.

They have an additional role to examine the patient in advance of the hearing if required and if practicable. This is called a pre-hearing examination (PHE). In Wales, PHEs are undertaken in all cases (Rule 20). In England, they are a requirement in s.2 cases and for patients subject to other sections, the patient or their legal representative must ask for a PHE and the request should be submitted 14 days ahead of the hearing date (Rule 34(1)). The examination is not a physical examination but a psychiatric examination and therefore based on discussion with the patient to establish their views and mental state.

The patient will have been given advance notice of the date and time of a PHE and should have the purpose of it explained beforehand. Where required, Medical Members must, as far as is practicable, examine the patient. This should take place in private and ahead of the hearing date, although, in practice, particularly in s.2 cases when hearings are listed at short notice, the PHE might take place shortly before the hearing.

The Medical Member can take *'such other steps as that member considers necessary to form an opinion of the patient's mental condition'*. They can *'examine records relating to the detention or treatment of the patient and any aftercare services'*. They can also *'take notes and copies of records for use in connection with the proceedings'* (Rule 34 (E), Rule 20 (W)). The Medical Member may also speak to ward staff as part of this process.

There is no obligation on the patient to cooperate with the PHE and the duty of the Medical Member to examine the patient is only as far as is practicable, which means, if a patient is unwilling to engage with the examination, then the hearing can still proceed without a PHE. In most cases it is probably in the patient's interests to meet with the Medical Member as most people find a one-to-one discussion easier to manage than the formality of the hearing itself. It also means that the Panel will have a good idea of the patient's position and their hopes for the hearing in advance, which might reduce the need for extensive questioning of the patient in the hearing itself.

The PHE findings will be shared with the other Panel Members before the hearing starts. However, it would be unfair for information that the Tribunal has heard not to be made available to the patient, their representative and others present at the hearing and therefore one of the first steps at a hearing is for a summary of the PHE to be shared with everyone in attendance. This allows for any dispute about what was said at the PHE or any significant difference between the medical evidence and the PHE findings to be addressed. The Medical Member is only entitled to form a provisional view and the Courts have held that expressing a concluded opinion before all of the evidence has been heard would make the proceedings unfair and unlawful (see, for example, *R (RD) v MHRT* [2007]). Sensible legal representatives will wish to hear the PHE feedback before making any opening remarks to ensure the patient's discussion with the Medical Member is not contradictory to their instructions to the representative.

FAQ: Why might a legal representative ask for a PHE? What happens if the patient refuses to be examined?

Answer: If the patient is doing well the legal representative may be keen for the Medical Member to see this. In addition, the representative may consider that the patient may express themselves more effectively in a one-to-one discussion with the Medical Member than during the hearing.

If the patient refuses to be seen by the Medical Member, then the PHE is not practicable and the hearing can proceed.

Role of the Specialist Lay Member

The SpLM's role is primarily to provide a view that is neither medical or legal, but focused on community, social and health services, aftercare and discharge options. As we have seen, the term 'lay' is a little misleading as SpLMs will likely bring a great deal of knowledge and relevant professional experience to the role.

The SpLM will focus on the social circumstances of the patient, likely aftercare and support available should they not be subject to the MHA and what services could be made available.

They should be familiar with the usual process for s.117 MHA aftercare planning and assessments for care and support under other relevant legislation. They will be well informed on issues relevant to social services such as child and adult safeguarding and the impact of mental disorder on the person and their family and community. All of which will inform their questioning of witnesses and the final decision making.

Independence of the Tribunal Panel

The Panel is entirely independent of the Responsible Authority (the hospital where the patient is detained or subject to a Community Treatment Order (CTO) or the Local Authority responsible if subject to Guardianship).

Hale (2007, p287) states:

> *It is an essential feature of a 'Court' for the purpose of a5(4) that it is separate from the detaining authorities but also that the individual members must be and must be seen to be impartial.*

Medical Members may also be Second Opinion Appointed Doctors (SOADs) with the Care Quality Commission (CQC) or Health Inspectorate Wales (HIW) and have visited patients in that role as well as meeting them at a Tribunal. There may be situations where Panel Members know professionals attending the hearing. These examples need not necessarily rule Panel Members out of hearing the case, but questions of actual or apparent bias are important in legal proceedings.

If anyone attending a hearing has a concern about possible bias, they should raise this as soon as possible. The Panel can then consider the issue and the parties can be consulted for their views on whether the fairness of the proceedings might be compromised.

FAQ: What is bias?

Answer: The answer is set out in case-law as follows:

The test for actual bias is whether the Tribunal Member is partial in the sense of favouring one side or being hostile to another. The test for the real possibility of bias is 'whether the fair-minded and informed observer, having considered the facts, would conclude that there was a real possibility that the Tribunal was biased' (Porter v Magill [2002]).

The Tribunal Clerk

Note that there may be a clerk at some Tribunals in England, but they are not usually clerked in Wales. Clerks are responsible for the administration of the hearing. Some hospitals provide in-house clerking, usually a member of the MHA Administration team. The role of Clerk is to ensure that proceedings are set up efficiently, that the Panel is made aware of who will attend, seating is arranged accordingly, all present have access to the relevant reports and any practical matters are dealt with. They will usually usher attendees in and out and chase up anyone who is absent or late. Where there is no clerk or assistance available to the Panel, this work will be done by the Panel Members.

Behind the scenes: The Tribunal Office

The Tribunal Office has administrative responsibility for the smooth running of the case from the point that an application or reference is submitted and will be responsible for checking the parties' availability; listing the hearing; sending out relevant information to the parties; and ensuring that the necessary reports and information are submitted within the relevant timescales and made available to the Panel. The Tribunal Office will chase late reports or documents and can issue directions and summonses in the event of continued non-compliance with time limits.

The Tribunal Office will also arrange for any interpreter or signer requested for the hearing and will notify the Nearest Relative (NR) of the patient of the Tribunal proceedings unless the patient has indicated that they object to the NR being notified of the proceedings on their application or reference.

The Tribunal operates a scheme of delegation so some legal decisions before the hearing (known as case management requests) can be dealt with by case workers or registrars. More complex legal decisions will be referred to a salaried Judge for determination. In Wales this will be the President or a Deputy of the President. Examples of case management requests would be seeking postponement of the hearing; seeking to withdraw the application; requesting that information be withheld from the patient; or asking for a time extension for reports to be filed.

Paper hearings

The general rule is that applications and references to the Tribunal must be dealt with by a 'hearing' which means a face-to-face hearing where the parties have the opportunity to present their case to the Tribunal in person. There is one exception to this rule in England: if a reference to the Tribunal has been made by the Hospital Managers under s.68 MHA in respect of a community patient (i.e. a patient on a CTO), then the patient (if they have capacity) or their representative can inform the Tribunal that they do not wish to attend the hearing or to be represented at a hearing. In these cases, there will be a paper review without the need for the patient or professionals to attend. The Tribunal will consider the reports and make a decision without hearing any oral evidence (see Rule 35 (E); there is no equivalent in the Welsh rules).

A patient may opt for a paper review if, for example, they were recalled to hospital and their CTO was revoked (which would trigger an automatic reference) but, by the time of the hearing, they have been discharged home on a new CTO and might now be disinterested in engaging with a hearing. As you might expect, it is almost certain that a paper review will result in the CTO continuing.

Top tips

- *There is no defined division of labour between Panel Members so you might be questioned in depth by any of the Panel Members.*

- *Remember that in England a CTO patient whose case has been referred to the Tribunal can request a 'paper review'. This can be requested by sending a Form T128 to the Tribunal Office.*

- *Case management requests that are submitted promptly and with well-drafted reasons are more likely to be agreed upon by the Tribunal Office.*

Chapter summary

- The Tribunal Panel is made up of three members, all of whom have to be in attendance at a hearing.

- The Judge will always chair proceedings.

- Medical Members may have met the patient in advance at a pre-hearing examination (PHE).

- Usually the Medical Member will lead the questioning of the Responsible Clinician and the SpLM will lead the questioning of the author of the social circumstances report.

- The Judge will often lead enquiries into the statutory grounds for detention, CTO or Guardianship.

- The Medical Member will enquire into the criteria, including mental disorder, nature, degree and risk criteria.

- The SpLM will enquire into the wider social circumstances of the patient and in particular what assistance might be required and available in the community should they be discharged from section.

- All Panel Members can ask questions of all professionals in attendance and of the patient.

Chapter 5
Who should attend the Tribunal hearing and why?

Introduction

This chapter will explain who attends the Tribunal and why. It will provide details of those who are permitted to attend, those who are required to attend and others who may attend. It will also explain what might happen if anyone is unable to or does not attend the hearing.

The Tribunal Panel

Chapter 4 looks in detail at the constitution of the Tribunal Panel. The Senior President of Tribunals has issued a practice statement defining the composition of Tribunals which *must* be:

- *one Judge; and*
- *one other member who is a registered medical practitioner; and*
- *one other member who has substantial experience in health or social care matters.*

(Practice Statement: Composition of Tribunals 2015)

Therefore a hearing could not proceed in the absence of one or more of the Panel Members.

General rules for professionals attending Tribunals

The general rule in Tribunal hearings is that a 'party to proceedings' is entitled to attend.

Where the Tribunal Rules refer to a 'party' this means the patient and the Responsible Authority. The Responsible Authority will be the hospital where the patient is either detained or was placed on a CTO or in cases where the patient is subject to Guardianship, the relevant Local Authority. Where the Nearest Relative (NR) has applied to the Tribunal, they are also a party.

In restricted cases the Secretary of State or the Welsh Ministers are also parties and could attend or be represented at a hearing, although this would be rare. We have also encountered the Secretary of State sending a representative to hearings where the Tribunal is considering sanctioning the removal of a patient to an overseas jurisdiction (see s.86 Mental Health Act (MHA)) – but this is also very rare.

Finally, a private Guardian (under the MHA), the Court of Protection (if there is a current Court order) and the Nearest Relative (NR) (even if they have not made the application) unless the patient has requested otherwise will all be treated as 'interested persons' and are entitled to be notified of and to take part in the Tribunal proceedings. The Tribunal also has the discretion to notify and hear from any other person they believe should be heard (Rule 33 (E), Rule 16 (W)).

Others in attendance will be witnesses on behalf of the Responsible Authority (for example, the Responsible Clinician (RC), inpatient nurse or Care Coordinator, who have, in most cases, prepared the relevant reports) and any independent experts. Other professionals may attend if they have knowledge that may be of assistance to the Responsible Authority's case or to the Tribunal generally. An example might be where the RC is not a doctor, but there are nevertheless issues about medication that require medical evidence. There may be others in attendance to offer the patient support and assistance (such as family members, carers or Independent Mental Health Advocates (IMHAs)) or those attending as observers.

An interpreter may be required to attend and the Tribunal Office will arrange this. In some cases, victims have rights to make limited representations concerning any conditions they feel should be attached to a discharge (see below).

The Rules give Tribunals a wide discretion to permit a person to attend or to exclude a person from part or the whole of a hearing if, for example, their presence was likely to be disruptive; would inhibit evidence of another; or lead to disclosure of information that has been withheld (Rule 38 (E), Rule 25 (W)). The decision on who attends and who is excluded rests with the Tribunal Panel, and the overarching principle that will be applied in these decisions is whether attendance or not would be in the interests of justice.

Finally, although the starting point is that Tribunal proceedings are held in private, it is possible for the patient to make an application for a public hearing. This would be very rare but there have been some successful applications, notably Ian Brady was permitted a public Tribunal hearing in 2011, and the media were able to observe via video-link (*Re Ian Brady* [2011]).

The patient

The overriding objective of the Tribunal includes ensuring, so far as practicable, that the parties are able to participate fully in the proceedings. In practice, this means that the patient should be enabled to attend, made to feel at their ease and as comfortable with the proceedings as is possible given the circumstances. Legal representatives would, in most cases, advise the patient that the prospects of securing discharge or some other positive outcome will be reduced if the Panel do not have the opportunity to meet and hear from the patient, and the representative should have spent time with the patient explaining the procedures and what to expect.

> *Normally patients will be present throughout hearings. Patients ... do not need to attend the Tribunal hearing, but professionals should encourage and support them to attend unless they judge that it would be detrimental to the patient's health or wellbeing.*
>
> *(Code 12.28 (E), 12.31 (W))*

If the patient does not attend the hearing?

The Rules permit a Tribunal hearing to proceed in the absence of a party if they are satisfied that the person was aware of the hearing (or reasonable steps have been taken to notify them), and it is in the interests of justice to proceed in their absence (Rule 39 (E), Rule 27 (W)). The English Rules also state that the Tribunal cannot proceed without the patient unless the pre-hearing medical examination has taken place where required and the patient has decided not to attend or is unable to attend for reasons of ill health.

Most commonly, this would arise if, for example, the patient becomes anxious about attending or their mental health has deteriorated or they are absent without leave on the day of the hearing. Judges will sometimes approach the *interests of justice* question by asking whether the patient would be more likely to be able to engage properly in the proceedings if the hearing were adjourned or whether it would make no difference.

CASE STUDY

Mr B

Mr B is currently absent without leave (AWOL) on the day of his s.3 hearing. Prior to this, Mr B had made an application to the Tribunal and appointed a legal representative. Mr B was made aware of the hearing both by the legal representative and the Hospital Managers. The legal representative had met with Mr B several weeks ago in preparation for the hearing. The legal representative is unable to take further instructions from Mr B since he went AWOL four days ago.

Question:

* *What might the Tribunal consider when deciding whether to proceed without Mr B or adjourn?*

Professionals required to attend

Hospital managers should ensure that all professionals who attend the Tribunal hearings are adequately prepared (Code 12.35 (E), 12.40 (W)). This means they should understand what is expected of them and the usual process during proceedings (i.e. who goes first, how to give evidence, likely questions they will be asked, etc.).

The authors of the relevant Tribunal reports should attend to speak to their written evidence, although it is not unusual for professionals who may not have written the report to attend the hearing on behalf of a colleague:

> *The Tribunal may ask the authors of the reports to talk through their report, so it is good practice for the authors to re-familiarise themselves with the content of any report before the hearing. If the author is unable to attend, it is important that*

anyone attending in their place should wherever possible also have good knowledge of the patient's case.

(Code 12.16 (E), 12.39 (W))

It is important that ... people who prepare reports submitted by the Responsible Authority attend the hearing to provide further up-to-date information about the patient, including (where relevant) their home circumstances and the aftercare available in the event of a decision to discharge the patient.

(Code 12.33 (E), 12.36 (W))

Table 5.1 sets out which professionals are required to attend. The chapter will then further explain others who may attend and why, before looking at what might happen if someone does not attend on the day. Professionals should be prepared to attend the full hearing.

Both the Welsh and English MHA Codes state that it is important the patient's RC attend the Tribunal supported by other staff involved in the patients care, as their evidence is crucial for making the case for a patient's continued detention or community compulsion under the Act. The Codes also indicate that wherever possible the staff should attend the full hearing so that they are aware of all the evidence made available to the Tribunal and the Tribunal's decision and reasons (Code 12.30 (E), 12.34 (W)).

Table 5.1   Which professionals are required to attend the Tribunal hearing?

Who should attend?	What is their role?
Responsible Clinician (RC)	To speak to the clinician's report and answer questions from the panel and the patient's representative. A more junior doctor might attend on the RC's behalf. Whichever clinician attends, they need to be prepared to be questioned on the statutory criteria that apply in each case. There may be a need to update the panel between the time of the report and the time of the hearing.
Nurse (for inpatients)	To speak to the nursing report, and answer questions from the panel and the patient's representative. This will usually be the nurse accompanying the patient from the ward. Ideally, the nurse should be able to answer questions on current progress and have seen the patient recently. Note that the English MHA Code states that *'increasingly Tribunal hearings find it helpful to speak to a nurse, particularly a nurse who knows the patient. It is often helpful for a nurse who knows the patient to accompany them.'* (Code 12.34). Again, any update on the situation between the date of the report and time of the hearing is an essential part of the evidence. NB: In Chapter 7b we look at the additional requirements in Wales for patients subject to CTO and Guardianship where a nurse might be present.

Who should attend?	What is their role?
Author of the social circumstances report (SCR)	To speak to the social circumstances report (SCR) and answer questions from the panel and from the patient's representative. Updating the panel on anything since the report was submitted. There may be times where the author of the SCR may also have been given a Facilities Report. See Chapter 7 for more details of Facilities Reports.
Patient's representative	In the majority of cases, the patient will have a legal representative to assist with presenting their case, assisting the patient to give their evidence; cross-examining the professional witnesses; and making closing submissions on behalf of the patient.
Representative for other parties	Another party such as the Nearest Relative (NR) in some cases may have their own legal representation at the Tribunal.
Independent Mental Health Advocate	IMHAs are not required to attend. However, their role is to support and assist the patient in understanding any issues arising and communicating with the panel (Practice Note: Role of the IMHA in First-tier Tribunal (Mental Health) Hearings 2011). The MHA Code for Wales (Para 6.8) makes the point that IMHAs have a specific advocacy role and are not there to be used as translators, interpreters or as providers of general communication support unless the circumstances are exceptional. See below for more details on the role of IMHAs in relation to Tribunals.
Interpreter	An interpreter to assist the patient is provided by the Tribunal service if required.
Independent experts	See Chapter 8. The patient may have instructed an independent expert to prepare a report and to attend the hearing to give evidence to challenge the professionals' evidence.

If a professional does not attend the hearing?

A failure by a professional to attend will be dealt with less sympathetically than the patient not attending and may lead to an adjournment and issuing of a summons. An element of a fair hearing under Article 6 ECHR is the right for a person to question or cross-examine witnesses. The absence of anyone to speak to the RC's report would almost certainly lead to an adjournment; however, there might be cases such as a s.2 hearing in respect of a patient not previously known to mental health services when the Tribunal may decide to proceed in the absence of a person to give social circumstances evidence if this evidence is likely to be limited and might make little difference to decisions on the criteria for detention. If it became apparent in the course of the hearing that the missing evidence might have a material effect on the Tribunal's decision making it would be open to the Tribunal to adjourn the hearing 'part heard', make directions for the missing evidence to be provided and, if possible, the next hearing will be with the same Panel Members because they will already have heard some of the evidence.

Dr S is the RC for Mrs C who is due to have a Tribunal hearing at the end of the week. Unfortunately, Dr S is unable to attend the hearing having just had confirmation of a hospital appointment.

Questions:

* *What are the consequences of Dr S not being able to attend the hearing and how should Dr S and the hospital manage this situation?*

See below for things to be considered in situations such as these.

In practice, any witnesses who cannot attend should have notified the Tribunal ahead of the hearing and perhaps have sought a postponement of the hearing to a different date if it was not possible to arrange another professional to cover the hearing. With the exception of s.2 cases which are listed very quickly, the hospital and patient's representative are required to confirm availability with the Tribunal to avoid this sort of difficulty arising.

Where a professional is unable to attend the full hearing, they should explain to the Tribunal when they need to leave. If there is a clerk present, it is best to notify them as soon as possible. A full explanation for why the professional is unable to attend the full hearing will be required. Ultimately the Tribunal has the discretion to decide whether or not to grant the request to leave early or arrive later in the proceedings but will generally be sympathetic to the demand of clinical work on professionals. Offering to leave contact details with the Panel in case something arises that requires the professional later in the hearing will usually assist with requests to leave after giving evidence.

EXPERT QUOTE

In a Tribunal hearing, you are a witness, and are giving evidence in Court. Your duty is to assist the Court and to enable the proceedings to achieve the overriding objective.

The patient's representative

The patient can appoint a representative to represent them in the proceedings. Given that non-means-tested Legal Aid is available to patients who wish to pursue an application to the Tribunal, it is likely that in the majority of cases the patient will be legally represented. The representative does not need to be legally qualified but mental health Legal Aid contracts require the representative attending a hearing to be a member of the Law Society's Mental Health Accreditation Scheme.

The Rules allow the Tribunal to appoint a legal representative for the patient if they have not appointed a representative for themselves and either lack capacity to appoint and it is in their best interests to be represented or do not wish to attend unrepresented (see Chapter 8).

The Tribunal requires written notice if a representative has been appointed. This could be anyone the patient wishes to appoint except that the Rules exclude a person who is also subject to the MHA or is receiving treatment for mental disorder at the same hospital as the patient (Rule 11, (E), Rule 13 (W)). In most cases the patient will be legally represented by a solicitor or suitably accredited trainee or paralegal from a law firm with a mental health Legal Aid contract. In preparation for the hearing the legal representative will (or certainly should) have interviewed the patient and taken initial instructions; considered the reports, section papers and medical and nursing notes; discussed and taken instructions from the patient on this information; and advised the patient on the merits of the case and the available applications that might be made to the Tribunal. The representative may also have discussed the case with the NR or any other person the patient wishes to attend the hearing or to give evidence and may have attended CPA/Care and Treatment Planning reviews/s.117 meetings or Hospital Managers' reviews in the course of the case.

A representative for another party

Any other party to proceedings is entitled to their own legal representation. For example, in situations where the Nearest Relative has used their power to apply directly to the Tribunal they may be represented independently of the patient's representative. It would be unusual, but the Responsible Authority may appoint a representative to assist the professional witnesses by, for example, asking questions and making legal submissions. This is only likely to arise in particularly contentious or high-profile cases.

The Independent Mental Health Act Advocate (IMHA)

Where the patient is eligible to have access to an IMHA they may attend the hearing to provide support to the patient. It is not usually the case that they provide representation, give evidence or ask questions of other witnesses, although in theory the patient could appoint them as a representative. The Welsh MHA Code (6.6) lists a range of situations in which an IMHA may assist the patient, including supporting the patient in applying to and obtaining legal representation for the MHRTW.

The English Tribunal produced a practice statement to clarify the role of IMHAs at Tribunal hearings. The Role of the Independent Mental Health Advocate in First-tier Tribunal (Mental Health) Hearings (May 2011) states that whilst an IMHA may be a 'representative' within the Tribunal Procedure Rules, the guidance is based on an expectation that ordinarily the IMHA 'should play a role distinct from the legal representative'. The guidance also states that the Tribunal should 'enable and support the IMHA in the discharge of his or her legitimate functions before the Tribunal'.

An IMHA can assist the patient in the lead up to the proceedings and attend to offer support and guidance during the hearing. They can assist the patient to voice their views but should guard against stepping into the role of the legal representative. The Judge may check with the IMHA and legal representative to clarify their roles ahead of the hearing.

The interpreter

As we saw in Chapter 1, the Tribunal is responsible for supplying interpreting services where they are made aware of the requirement. The Responsible Authority should ensure they are given adequate notice of the need for any specialist language, signing or interpretation. This is provided free of charge by the Tribunal.

The MHRTW has a Welsh-language scheme. The Tribunal will ensure that hearings can be held in Welsh if that is the patient's language of choice. Interpreters are provided free of charge by the Tribunal. The interpreter will meet with the patient ahead of the hearing and will sit beside the patient at the hearing.

Other professionals

There could be a range of professionals or agencies attending to give evidence to the Tribunal. It might be important for the Tribunal to hear evidence from a housing department or housing provider on issues related to future planning with a view to discharge.

Social Services departments such as children's services might attend in the case of a patient under the age of 18 with a view to giving further information on discharge plans, child protection and safeguarding issues.

It is also open to the Tribunal to use their case management powers to direct the attendance of a particular professional if their evidence is likely to be of assistance to the Tribunal's decision making.

Other non-professionals

NRs, family and friends: if the NR has not actually applied to the Tribunal directly, they may still be in attendance to either offer support or as a witness to give evidence. Similarly, family and friends who attend will need to confirm whether they intend to be there in a supportive capacity (in which case they will not be speaking) or to offer evidence or information to assist the Tribunal.

The patient is entitled to bring another along with them to provide support (not a representative). Those doing so can attend without giving advance notice to the Tribunal but will need permission from the Panel on the day. They are not permitted to take notes or give evidence but can offer emotional and moral support to the patient during the proceedings.

Victims

As a result of the Domestic Violence, Crime and Victims Act 2004, victims of some sexual or violent offences are entitled to be informed of Tribunal proceedings. This will be done via the Victim Liaison Officer (VLO) in the relevant probation service for restricted cases or via the Hospital Managers for unrestricted cases. The relevant circumstances are where the patient is subject to a hospital order (with or without restrictions) a trans-fer direction or a hybrid order. The victim is entitled to make representations concerning whether in the event of discharge the patient should be subject to conditions and if so, what those conditions should be. Victims may make such representations via the VLO for restricted patients or in writing to the Hospital Managers for unrestricted patients.

Victims could also apply to attend a hearing as a person who should *'have the opportunity of being heard'* under the Rules. However, a victim is not a 'party' and it would be very unusual circumstances that attending a hearing would be seen as being in the interests of justice and the English Tribunal's practice guidance states:

> *Direct involvement in the proceedings, or a procedure that brings the victim into direct conflict with the patient, is unlikely to be helpful to the victim, to the patient, or to the Tribunal.*

> *(Practice Guidance on Procedures Concerning Handling Representations from Victims in the First-tier Tribunal (Mental Health) 2011, p4)*

The English and Welsh Codes of Practice have further general guidance on managing contact with the patient and support for victims who are family members, carers or friends (Code 40.21–40.23 (E), 40.23–40.26 (W)).

Observers

Some observations will generally be facilitated when they are for the induction of new Tribunal Members or for appraisals of current members.

Any planned observation for Tribunal Members' induction or appraisal purposes will be booked in advance and the Tribunal and others made aware. They take no part in the questioning or deliberations but can make confidential notes for the purposes of their observations, and they are allowed to see the reports. The parties are not required to consent to this procedure, but even so the Tribunal may decide not to continue with the observation if the presence of the observer might cause a patient distress, for example.

Other observations that might be facilitated include a range of professionals who need to observe a hearing as part of their learning and development. For example, and most likely, student nurses, social workers, occupational therapists, psychologists or junior doctors as well as legal representatives who are seeking accreditation with the Law Society.

Guidance from the Tribunal (Guidance for the Observation of Tribunal Hearings in the First-tier Tribunal Health Education and Social Care Chamber (Mental Health Jurisdiction) 10 January 2019) states that such observations should assist the observer in becoming a more effective witness or representative in the future.

The same guidance provides details for the Tribunal Members on when and in what circumstances an observer may attend a hearing to observe the process. In summary the Rules for all observers are as follows:

The Tribunal decides whether or not anyone can observe the hearing. Ideally these requests should be made in advance but can be considered on the day. The patients' views should always be taken as well as the views of other parties before granting or refusing a request to observe and it would be highly unusual for an observer to be permitted in the face of a patient's objection.

The Panel will need to consider whether anything might impact on the ability of any party to fully participate and whether the presence of an observer would be likely to cause distress to the patient. They are also entitled to consider the practical impact of an additional person in the Tribunal hearing and whether or not it may have an adverse impact on the fairness or smooth running of the hearing.

Where an application to observe is granted, the following rules apply:

- Reports will be not disclosed to them.

- They will be advised that the proceedings are confidential and information about the proceedings must not be made public by the observer.

- They may take notes for observation purposes but these notes are confidential.

- They may not contribute to any questioning during the hearing.

- They are not entitled to remain for the deliberations by the Tribunal.

The MHRTW website states that anyone wishing to observe the hearing would be required to complete form MHRTW-02 in advance of the hearing.

> ### EXPERT QUOTE
>
> *Make sure that you have witnessed a Tribunal prior to having to attend in person to give evidence.*

Excluding people from the hearing

The Tribunal may determine who is permitted to attend the hearing or part of it. On the rare occasions that a Tribunal is held in public the Rules specify that the Tribunal may direct that part of the hearing is to be held in private.

The Rules (38 (E) and 25 (W)) provide powers to the Tribunal to exclude any person (including the patient) from all or part of a hearing where there is concern that their presence would be disruptive, inhibit another person's evidence or would cause difficulty in respect of a non-disclosure issue. The English Rules also provide for exclusion of a person if their presence would defeat the purpose of the hearing.

The Tribunal Panel will make all reasonable adjustments for the patient and take account of the overriding objective to deal with the case fairly and justly. As we saw in Chapter 1, they will avoid unnecessary formality and seek flexibility in the proceedings to ensure the patient and others are able to participate fully. However, there may be times where the patient is unable to manage the proceedings without becoming anxious or agitated, and consequently disruptive, or otherwise affecting the hearing.

The Tribunal could exclude a witness from the hearing except for when they are giving their evidence, and it might be that excluding the patient from part of or all of the proceedings is unavoidable. A patient could be excluded if their behaviour is preventing the case from being properly heard or presenting a risk to other attendees. This would be unusual and our experience has been that Panels will go to great lengths to try and ensure that the patient is able to participate as fully as possible. Patient's representatives will try and assist the patient to manage the potential stress of the hearing and might suggest the patient be given the opportunity to deal with their evidence at the beginning of the hearing. If there are concerns about the patient's presentation or ability to cope with the hearing, professionals may wish to consider raising this with the Panel as a preliminary issue before the full hearing starts and also to consider carefully the most appropriate venue for the hearing. Hearings will sometimes be held on wards rather than in administrative parts of the hospital to ensure that there are nursing staff available to deal with any risk or absconsion concerns.

The Practice Direction requires authors of reports to explain any factors that they think may affect the patient's ability to cope with a hearing and whether there are any adjustments professionals consider the Tribunal may consider in order to deal with the case fairly and justly.

Top tips

- *If you are the author of the report try to ensure you are able to attend the hearing.*

- *In situations where your absence is unavoidable, ensure that a colleague is brought up-to-date with the case, information in your report and the reasons for your recommendations.*

- *If you wish to observe a hearing, be aware that you may not be able to do so on the day and the final decision rests with the Tribunal who will usually seek the agreement of the patient.*

- *It is advisable to check who will be in attendance ahead of the actual hearing as part of the professionals' preparation for the hearing.*

- *If you have concerns about the patient or any other person planning to attend the hearing, do let the Tribunal know at the earliest opportunity.*

- *We would recommend that any junior doctors, students or uninitiated professionals take the opportunity to observe at least one hearing before they are required to attend as a witness.*

Chapter summary

- The Tribunal decides who attends and who may be excluded.

- The parties are entitled to attend.

- The patient is not required to attend but should be encouraged and enabled to attend wherever possible.

- The authors of the reports should attend.

- Where the authors of the reports cannot attend, a substitute should be available who can speak to the written evidence and add their own recommendations and information.

- In most cases a legal representative will attend.

- There may be more than one legal representative if the Nearest Relative has applied in their own right.

Chapter 6
How do Tribunals apply the law?

Introduction

This chapter will seek to demystify elements of the Tribunal hearing by explaining the legal tests that are in the minds of the Panel and therefore why particular lines of questioning of the professionals are likely to be pursued by the Panel or the legal representative. At a hearing, you are likely to hear the phrases *'statutory criteria'* or *'legal grounds'*, or reference to the specific part of the statute under consideration, for example, *'the s.72 criteria'*. These terms all mean the same thing and simply refer to the legal questions that a Tribunal must ask and make findings on in a particular case. If a Tribunal is not satisfied that any of the criteria continue to be met they are under a positive duty to discharge.

As a starting point it might be of some reassurance to professionals to know that the criteria being applied by the Tribunal largely mirror the criteria for admission under section which readers may be more familiar with. There is a subtle difference in that Tribunals are considering the potential consequences of discharge from detention in a hospital setting (or discharge from community compulsion) rather than whether the patient meets the grounds for admission in the first place. The Courts have consistently recognised this distinction and that patients detained in the contained environment of a hospital are in a very different position from patients in the community. This is why Jones (2020, p462) says:

> *The patient's RC should not be asked: 'Would the patient's current mental state justify making an application?'. Rather, she should be asked to identify the consequences for the patient and/or the public if the Tribunal decided to discharge the patient.*

As with the rest of the book, this chapter uses the term Responsible Clinician (RC) when discussing the medical evidence, but, of course, it may not be the RC giving the oral evidence at a hearing and this role will often be delegated to a Core or Specialist Trainee Psychiatrist. The RC may also be a non-medic such as a psychologist.

As you look at the legal criteria that are applied by a Tribunal, you will not see any references to the patient's human rights or to the language found in Article 5 of the European Convention on Human Rights (ECHR) or European Court of Human Rights (ECtHR) case-law. This is because the Courts have said on a number of occasions (including the PJ case discussed in Chapter 11) that human rights matters are implicit within the legal tests that the Tribunal apply and they cannot apply any criteria not expressly set out in the MHA.

The legal criteria for the Tribunal to consider are found in Part V of the Mental Health Act (MHA) and professionals will most likely be dealing with cases under s.72 MHA, which covers s.2, s.3, CTO, unrestricted hospital order and Guardianship cases. There are separate sections covering restricted patients and patients transferred from prison, which are considered in more detail below.

As discussed in Chapter 1, remember that, in most cases, the 'burden' is on the detaining authority to satisfy the Tribunal that the grounds for continued detention or compulsion are met. In relation to the legal criteria the focus will usually be on the RC's evidence, although nursing staff or care coordinators might also be asked to express a view – especially if they know the patient well.

At the beginning of the hearing, Judges might seek to 'narrow the issues' in dispute by asking the patient or their legal representative whether any of the criteria are conceded and then asking the RC to confirm which grounds are being relied on for the detention to continue. So, for example, a patient might say that they accept their diagnosis and therefore are not contesting whether there is a mental disorder or not, but they feel that they have improved to the point that they can safely continue treatment in the community and therefore their detention is no longer 'necessary'. Equally, an RC might concede that the patient has improved and their mental disorder is no longer of a 'degree', but there is something about the 'nature' of the disorder that makes continued detention appropriate. Having confirmed the statutory criteria being relied on by the RC, most Judges will then hand over to the Medical Member of the Tribunal to deal with more detailed questioning of the RC.

Narrowing the issues can assist the hearing process a great deal as, although the Tribunal have to make their own independent findings, if something is uncontested, then it may be that questions on this point can be limited and more focus given to the issues in dispute. This might be particularly helpful for the patient as they probably will not be quizzed about something they are not disputing (see Chapter 9).

Although there are differences in the precise wording of the criteria depending on the section, there are key legal terms that are common to almost all Tribunal cases and these will usually be the initial questions to the RC.

Mental disorder

Is there a mental disorder at all? If there is no mental disorder, then the MHA does not apply. It would be unusual for a Tribunal to find that a patient is not suffering from any mental disorder, but it can happen – particularly in s.2 cases when there may be no prior history of contact with mental health services and the patient perhaps argues that the presentation that led to their admission was caused by something other than a mental disorder – for example, intoxication, bereavement or some other significant stressor.

Section 1(2), MHA defines mental disorder as:

> *Any disorder or disability of the mind.*

This is a very wide definition indeed. It is a legal definition and a condition does not need to be listed in any of the diagnostic manuals such as the *International Classification of Diseases (ICD) 11* to be a mental disorder for the purposes of the s.1 definition and, conversely, a condition being listed in a manual does not necessarily make it a mental disorder for the purposes of s.1. Para 2.5 of the MHA Code has a helpful list of recognised mental disorders which could be within the s.1 definition and are the conditions you will most likely encounter in Tribunal proceedings:

- *Affective disorders, such as depression and bipolar disorder*

- *Schizophrenia and delusional disorders*

- *Neurotic, stress-related and somatoform disorders, such as anxiety*

- *Phobic disorders, obsessive compulsive disorders, post-traumatic stress disorder and hypochondriacal disorders*

- *Organic mental disorders such as dementia and delirium (however caused)*

- *Personality and behavioural changes caused by brain injury or damage (however acquired)*

- *Personality disorders*

- *Mental and behavioural disorders caused by psychoactive substance use*

- *Eating disorders, non-organic sleep disorders and non-organic sexual disorders*

- *Learning disabilities*

- *Autistic spectrum disorders (including Asperger's syndrome)*

- *Behavioural and emotional disorders of children and young people*

There are some specific exclusions:

> *s.1(3) Dependence on alcohol or drugs is not considered to be a disorder or disability of the mind.*

This exclusion is not straightforward because a person may have a separate mental disorder in addition to drug or alcohol dependence, or the drug and alcohol use may have given rise to a mental disorder – examples would be drug-induced psychosis or Korsakoff's Syndrome. These types of cases would fall within the s.1 definition of mental disorder.

Learning disability is defined in s.1(4) as 'a state of arrested or incomplete development of the mind which includes significant impairment of intelligence and social functioning'. But there is a further limitation on this definition because, for the longer-term sections of the MHA, a learning disability is *not* considered to be a mental disorder unless it is 'associated with abnormally aggressive or seriously irresponsible conduct' (s.1(2A)).

Nature or degree

The presence of a mental disorder is obviously not sufficient in itself to permit detention in hospital. Mental disorders are common and most people are not admitted to hospital. The disorder has to be severe enough to justify the use of the MHA and it is the nature or degree of the disorder that is the legal test in most cases.

Degree simply means the current presentation, so professionals are likely to be asked questions about the signs, symptoms and manifestations of the disorder that the patient is *currently* exhibiting. Nature relates to the course of the disorder in the past, present and future, so likely questions will be about past responses to treatment, previous relapses and prognosis (see Code 14.6 (E), 14.5 (W)). Medical evidence regarding the nature of a disorder will often include phrases such as chronic, long-standing, relapsing and remitting, treatment-resistant, etc.

Note that the term is 'nature *or* degree' not 'nature *and* degree'. Only one of the tests has to be satisfied for the legal threshold for detention to be met, and professionals do not have to argue for both, although in many cases both nature and degree will be relevant. This also means that an asymptomatic patient may still not be discharged if their mental disorder is found to be of a nature to make their detention appropriate, although in these sorts of cases there is likely to be particular scrutiny of the evidence for the nature of the disorder and its relationship to any risks.

ACTIVITY 6.1

Read the cases below. What questions might you have for professionals about 'nature' and 'degree' and associated risk if you were a Panel Member?

Mr D

Mr D is detained under s.3 and has been in hospital for three months. His diagnosis is paranoid schizophrenia which is complicated by substance misuse and this is his seventh admission in the last five years. His mental state has improved a great deal with regular medication and nursing care and he is no longer showing any of the obvious signs of psychosis that were very evident on admission. Despite the improvement, Mr D's RC remains concerned that he is only cooperating with treatment because he is detained, he has no insight into his mental health needs, expresses a determination to continue using substances and the incidents of aggression prior to admissions appear to be becoming more serious on each occasion. The RC feels that discharge needs to be carefully planned and gradual to allow for some testing out in the community and that there is scope for further work to be done around Mr D's insight and his understanding of the role of drug use in his relapses. At the Tribunal, the RC argues that Mr D has a mental disorder that is of a nature but not currently of a degree to make continued detention appropriate.

Mrs E

Mrs E is detained under s.2 and has been in hospital for ten days. She has no history of contact with mental health services and there is little information available from her GP or family. She is presenting as very disturbed on the ward and her team suspect some sort of manic episode which requires further assessment, including a trial of medication. At the Tribunal, her RC argues that Mrs E has a mental disorder that is of a degree to warrant her detention. The RC does not rely on the nature of the disorder because of the lack of history and uncertainty about diagnosis and prognosis.

Health or safety or the protection of others

So, for detention to be lawful, there must be a mental disorder, and it must be serious enough either in its current presentation or looking at the course of the disorder over time. This is still not sufficient and:

> *There must be an element of risk to the patient or to others if the patient is not detained.*

> *(Hale, 2010, p57)*

Often referred to in shorthand as the 'risk criteria', the Tribunal is required to consider the risks that may or may not arise in the event of a patient being discharged from detention. This assessment of risk is probably the key issue in most Tribunals, and therefore you will find that questions from legal representatives will often be to try and make the case that any risk concerns can be managed less restrictively and without the need for continued detention. Also note that any risks must have some connection with the mental disorder; otherwise, they are irrelevant to the legal criteria and the Tribunal's decision making (*R(on the Application of Li) v MHRT* [2004]).

In the context of mental health work, the assessment of risk is difficult and hard to quantify as practitioners are seeking to predict a range of possible future outcomes. The Courts have, to an extent, recognised this inherent uncertainty and a Tribunal will not require absolute precision from professionals about the concerns for a patient's health or safety or for others as long as the risk assessment is rational. However, if particular past events are being relied on as part of the risk assessment, then the Tribunal will need to be satisfied on the balance of probabilities that those events did, in fact, happen and the more serious the alleged incident, the better the evidence will need to be to support the allegation.

If a particular ground is relied on to support continued detention, professionals are likely to be asked about previous history and any earlier examples of the particular risk and may be asked about the sources of the information (especially for serious allegations). This is why it is important to reference your sources in the written reports and, if possible, provide the context for any previous risk incidents (see Chapter 7). Comments such as 'history of assault' without further detail are quite likely to be challenged by the Tribunal or the legal representative.

Note that it is health *or* safety *or* the protection of others. There is no need to try and demonstrate evidence of risk in all three categories if you are arguing for detention or community compulsion to continue. Also note that we have not mentioned the word 'danger' or 'dangerous' – these terms do not exist in the statutory criteria except in the very specific case of a Nearest Relative (NR) Tribunal application after a barring order (see Chapter 2). The patient being *a danger to themselves or to others* is legally inaccurate and unhelpful because it may lead to professionals applying an artificially high-risk threshold when making decisions under the MHA.

There is no legal mystery in the terms *health, safety, protection of others*; they are ordinary words although there can be some blurring of boundaries, for example, a serious failure to manage physical health might compromise the patient's safety as well or a patient's behaviour that puts their own safety at risk may also indirectly give rise to concerns about the safety of others. Each term merits some further examination.

Health

This covers both the patient's physical and mental health. Physical health risks probably need no further explanation and might include self-neglect, malnutrition, dehydration or failure to manage other physical health matters due to the effect of the mental disorder. The MHA Codes (14.9 (E), 14.8 (W)) detail factors to consider in decisions to detain on the basis of health or safety concerns and, in respect of the patient's health, mention (to paraphrase):

- Self-neglect or inability to look after their own health;

- Jeopardising their own health accidentally, recklessly or unintentionally;

- Their mental disorder is otherwise putting their health at risk;

- Evidence that their mental health will deteriorate without treatment (including the views of the patient, carers, relatives, close friends);

- Their skills and experience to manage their condition;

- Capacity and consent issues;

- History, prognosis and the reliability of any evidence;

- Benefits of treatment v adverse effects of detention.

Safety

Safety concerns will probably be more obvious when considering a patient's case and may include risks arising from direct acts such as suicide attempts or self-harm, but 'safety' also covers indirect risks such as retaliatory harm (e.g. the patient being at risk of assault from others because of their conduct when floridly unwell) or an inability to keep themselves safe from the actions of others (e.g. placing themselves in abusive situations or relationships). More general safety concerns may also be relevant so, for example, if the mental disorder gives rise to cognitive or concentration difficulties, then there might be concerns about road safety or wandering.

Protection of others

Again, most risks to others will be fairly obvious to professionals considering a patient's case and will, of course, include violence, aggression and any relevant previous convictions.

The risks could be to a particular individual or to the wider public and this ground includes the risk of psychological as well as physical harm. The risks to others may also be indirect or unintentional, for example, a patient in a manic state who intends to continue driving or patients with parental or caring responsibilities whose ability to provide adequate care might be impaired by mental disorder.

The MHA Codes do not specify examples of behaviours giving rise to concerns about the protection of others but do give some general guidance on factors to consider (14.10 (E), 14.9 (W)), including:

- *Likelihood and severity of harm.*

- *It may not be possible to differentiate risk of harm to the patient from the risk to others.*

- *Reliability of evidence, past history, contact with other agencies.*

- *Willingness of those living with or providing care to the patient to manage the risks.*

- *Are there alternatives to detention to manage the risks?*

FAQ: Does the detention criteria mention 'danger to self or others'?

Answer: No. This is a common myth. Danger and dangerousness have a higher threshold than the admission criteria above. See below for more details on when this criterion is applied.

Appropriate medical treatment

This is an additional criterion that you will find in most of the longer-term sections. The underlying principle being that it would be unlawful to detain someone in hospital simply to contain them; there must be access to medical treatment for mental disorder at the hospital the patient is detained in. Tribunal cases will often be focused on the role of medication, but the definition of appropriate medical treatment is much wider, and you will find the definitions in s.145(1) and s.145(4) of the MHA:

Medical treatment:

> *includes nursing, psychological intervention and specialist mental health habilitation, rehabilitation and care.*

And appropriate medical treatment is medical treatment:

> *the purpose of which is to alleviate, or prevent a worsening of, the disorder or one or more of its symptoms or manifestations.*

A patient's refusal to comply or engage is not relevant – the treatment is still 'available'. The treatment does not have to be optimal, although it should be consistent with clinical guidelines (e.g. National Institute for Health and Care Excellence (NICE)). Note also that the requirement is that the *'purpose'* must be to alleviate, or prevent etc. – it is not necessary for clinicians to show in advance that a particular outcome will be achieved (Code 23.4 (E), 23.3(W)).

Because the definition of treatment is so broad, it would be extremely difficult for a patient to successfully argue that they should be discharged on the basis that this part of the legal criteria is not met. However, Tribunals may have questions about the treatment plan, its effectiveness and any adverse effects. Medical Members of the Tribunal in particular might have queries about why particular treatment approaches have been tried or not tried.

> *EXPERT QUOTE*
>
> *An example of a patient not being offered suitable treatment may be where a patient has a personality disorder but the ward has no current access to a clinical psychologist. Or a patient with a LD or ASD where the nursing staff have no specialist training in these conditions.*

Mental disorder, nature, degree, health, safety and protection of others will be the key themes and areas of dispute in almost all Tribunal hearings. There are some variations and additions in the criteria depending on the section that the patient is subject to, which we will consider in more detail. Each section begins with the exact wording of the statutory provision that the Tribunal will be considering.

Is 'insight' one of the legal tests?

You may hear the term 'insight' referred to at Tribunals and, indeed, the English and Welsh Practice Directions integrate it into their headings alongside capacity. Insight is not within the legal test in s.72, nor does it appear anywhere else in the Mental Health Act, and there is no reference to insight in either the current Welsh or English MHA Codes of Practice. Dictionary references to 'insight' include 'understanding', 'capacity', and the Cambridge Online Dictionary refers to insight as *'the ability to have a clear, deep and sometimes sudden understanding of a complicated problem or situation'* (https://dictionary.cambridge.org/dictionary/english/insight).

The problem with 'insight' is that we all have different views about it, and if it is applied to our own situations, we are all capable of at least a little denial and lack of insight. Its common use in Tribunals as 'evidence' of the need for continued detention needs to be clearly linked to the statutory criteria. Insight places the 'burden' on the patient. By failing to have gained insight or sufficient insight, the chances of discharge from detention or compulsion are presumably lowered, and all this even when insight is not within the legal criteria.

Insight remains legally ill-defined and its frequent use as an extra-legislative crite-rion threatens legal safeguards. There is a risk, in other words, that clinical concepts like insight might become proxy or substitute criteria for legal decisions.

(Allen, 2009, p165)

However, over ten years after that article was written, the term 'insight' is still used regularly at Tribunals, in the context of progress or understanding (or lack of) of illness and the need for treatment.

This is a practical guide rather than a critical analysis of Tribunals. Having said that, we believe there is scope for the Tribunal to review the emphasis on 'insight' and question authors who refer to it regularly by asking them what they mean and in what context. Use of 'insight' as 'evidence' of a continued requirement for detention or compulsion should be questioned. How long does it take an average person to 'gain insight'? Is 'insight' simply agreeing with the hospital team? Is developing insight a prerequisite to a patient being discharged from detention? What about a situation where someone never shifts in their opposition to the clinical team's views?

Section 2: Admission for assessment (s.72(1)(a))

(a)   *the Tribunal shall direct the discharge of a patient liable to be detained under section 2 above if it is not satisfied:*

  (i)   *that he is then suffering from mental disorder or from mental disorder of a nature or degree which warrants his detention in a hospital for assessment (or for assessment followed by medical treatment) for at least a limited period; or*

  (ii)   *that his detention as aforesaid is justified in the interests of his own health or safety or with a view to the protection of other persons …*

You will see that all of the key terms considered above are in the legal test – except that there is no requirement for appropriate medical treatment to be available because the purpose of s.2 is primarily for assessment.

Section 3: Admission for treatment and unrestricted hospital orders (s.72(1)(b))

(b)   *the Tribunal shall direct the discharge of a patient liable to be detained otherwise than under section 2 above if it is not satisfied:*

  (i)   *that he is then suffering from mental disorder or from mental disorder of a nature or degree which makes it appropriate for him to be liable to be detained in a hospital for medical treatment; or*

  (ii)   *that it is necessary for the health of safety of the patient or for the protection of other persons that he should receive such treatment; or*

  (iia)   *that appropriate medical treatment is available for him.*

At first glance, this looks very similar to the s.2 criteria above, but on closer examination you will see the references to medical treatment rather than assessment and also the use of the word 'necessary' in relation to the risk criteria. It is generally considered that 'necessary' slightly raises the legal threshold for continued detention because for something to be necessary there really cannot be any less restrictive way of providing treatment and managing the relevant risks. You will also see the additional requirement for appropriate treatment being available for this category of cases.

In s.3 cases only, if an NR has ordered discharge and been 'barred' by the RC (see Chapter 3), they are entitled to make their own application to the Tribunal independently of the patient's rights. If this happens, then the Tribunal has to consider an additional higher legal test:

> (iii) *in the case of an application by virtue of paragraph (g) of section 66(1) above, that the patient, if released, would be likely to act in a manner dangerous to other persons or to himself.*

This is the only circumstance when the phrase 'dangerous' arises in Tribunal proceedings. 'Dangerous' is evidently a higher level of risk than 'necessary for the health of safety of the patient or for the protection of other persons'. If not satisfied that this higher test is met, then the Tribunal must discharge even if the other criteria are met. Therefore, families are entitled to decide to take a limited level of risk in respect of the patient even in the face of conflicting professional opinion.

Section 17A: Community Treatment Orders (s.72(1)(c))

(c) *the Tribunal shall direct the discharge of a community patient if it is not satisfied:*

> (i) *that he is then suffering from mental disorder or mental disorder of a nature or degree which makes it appropriate for him to receive medical treatment; or*
>
> (ii) *that it is necessary for his health or safety or for the protection of other persons that he should receive such treatment; or*
>
> (iii) *that it is necessary that the Responsible Clinician should be able to exercise the power under section 17E(1) above to recall the patient to hospital; or*
>
> (iv) *that appropriate medical treatment is available for him.*

The legal criteria for CTO cases are very similar to those for s.3 (above) because, of course, there is a s.3 (or s.37) underlying the CTO. The differences are that the reference to 'liable to be detained' is removed because the patient is in the community, and there is the additional criterion of the necessity for the RC's recall power, which is probably the issue argued over most in CTO Tribunal hearings and both the Panel and legal representative are likely to ask questions to establish why the recall power is necessary over and above the existing powers to re-admit a patient under s.2 or s.3 for example (MHA Code 29.16 (E), 29.10 (W)).

The 'dangerous' criteria for Nearest Relative applications discussed above also apply to CTO cases.

Section 7 and 37: Guardianship orders (s.72(4))

(4)   *... and shall so direct if it is satisfied:*

   (a)   *that he is not then suffering from mental disorder; or*

   (b)   *that it is not necessary in the interests of the welfare of the patient, or for the protection of other persons, that the patient should remain under such Guardianship.*

Note the slightly different wording in this test which says, *'is satisfied ...'* rather than *'... not satisfied'*. This means that in Guardianship cases, the burden remains on the patient to show that the grounds are not met as opposed to most cases when the burden is on the detaining authority to show that the grounds *are* met.

The criteria in these cases are somewhat softened by the removal of the nature or degree requirements and by the introduction of the 'welfare of the patient', which is a much broader term than 'health or safety' of the patient. There is no reference to medical treatment because Guardianship tends to be used for more general protective purposes such as to ensure residence at a particular place and are unlikely to be appropriate if a key element of the patient's care plan is compliance with medication, for example.

Recommendations (s.72(3) and s.72(3A))

For all of the above categories of case, if not minded to discharge, the Tribunal also has the power to make statutory recommendations regarding leave of absence, transfer to another hospital or transfer into Guardianship. There are no defined legal criteria for making such a recommendation except that the recommendation can only be made for the purpose of *facilitating discharge on a future date*. If the patient is seeking a statutory recommendation, they will have to show that the recommendation will somehow advance them along their care pathway towards eventual discharge.

If the Tribunal thinks that the patient could be discharged under a CTO rather than remain detained in hospital, the statute says that there is no duty to discharge in these circumstances, and the Tribunal should instead consider making a statutory recommendation that the RC consider whether to make a CTO. The wording of s.72(3A) is a little odd because if the Tribunal did discharge in these circumstances, then the possibility of a CTO would disappear anyway.

Section 37/41: Restriction orders (s.73)

The criteria in restriction order cases are exactly the same as for s.3 (above) with an additional legal question and that is whether:

(b)   *the Tribunal is satisfied that it is not appropriate for the patient to remain liable to be recalled to hospital for further treatment.*

So, if the Tribunal is not satisfied that the grounds for detention are met they then have to decide whether a continuing recall power is appropriate when the patient leaves hospital. If the Tribunal does not think a recall power is necessary, they must grant an absolute discharge which means the patient is discharged without being subject to any legal framework. Restricted patients have committed a potentially serious offence leading to their detention in hospital by order of the Crown Court with a restriction order primarily for the protection of the public and therefore absolute discharges from hospital are rare.

If the Tribunal takes the view that the grounds for detention are not met but the liability to be recalled is appropriate, then they must grant a conditional discharge. See Chapter 3 for details of the conditions that can be imposed.

Section 45A, 47/49, 48/49: Restriction and limitation directions (s.74)

See Chapter 3 for a detailed discussion of the powers available to the Tribunal. You may recall that, in these cases (where the patient also remains a prisoner), the Tribunal has no power to discharge the patient and undertakes a slightly abstract exercise of treating the case as though the patient were detained under s.37/41, and then deciding whether they would be entitled to an absolute or conditional discharge and notifying the Secretary of State accordingly. The patient's eventual release will be governed by the Secretary of State or, more likely, the Parole Board. Therefore, the legal criteria that are considered at these hearings are exactly the same as for s.37/41 cases discussed above.

Conditionally discharged restricted patients (s.75)

A patient who is granted a conditional discharge and is released from detention in hospital is entitled to apply to the Tribunal after 12 months for an absolute discharge or for the conditions to be varied. In practice, there is an unwritten expectation that a patient is able to demonstrate a much longer period than 12 months in the community without any adverse events because ending the restriction order means that the patient is subject to no legal framework, conditions or liability to recall and the original order will have been imposed by the Court on the basis of a potentially serious offence.

Along with patients subject to Guardianship, this is the other category of cases where the 'burden' remains on the patient to show that the restriction order should end or the conditions should be varied or removed.

There are no statutory criteria to be applied in these cases, leaving decisions at the discretion of the Tribunal. In forming a judgement as to whether the power of recall remains appropriate or not, Tribunals can consider issues that would be within the criteria for a restricted patient, such as mental disorder, nature, degree, etc. (see above), but are not bound by them. However, case-law (see: *R(on the application of SC) v Mental Health Review Tribunal and the Secretary of State for Health* [2005]) has established a number of matters that are relevant in these cases and, in practice, many Tribunals will use them as an almost statutory set of criteria and may expect a legal representative to deal with them expressly. These are:

- The nature, gravity and circumstances of the index offence (the offence that led to the restriction order being made by the Court);

- The nature and gravity of the mental disorder in the past, present and future;

- The risk and likelihood of re-offending;

- The degree of harm to which the public would be exposed in the event of re-offending;

- The risk and likelihood of a recurrence or exacerbation of any mental disorder;

- The risk and likelihood of the need for recall in the future for further treatment in hospital;

- The reasons for the conditions that were imposed on the patient's release from hospital and the extent to which it is desirable to continue, vary or add to them.

These criteria are also reflected in the Practice Direction requirements for reports (see Chapter 7).

Finally, remember that as well as the Tribunal's powers in respect of all restricted patients, the Secretary of State has the discretion to grant an absolute discharge under s.42 MHA. It would be very rare for the Secretary of State to grant an absolute discharge and the only cases we have encountered in practice are when the patient is terminally ill.

Top tips

- *It is worth reminding yourself of the specific criteria that will be being considered before you walk in to a hearing. This might make you feel more confident in answering questions and will help your evidence to be legally accurate.*

- *A checklist might be of assistance in particular to the RC and you may notice Tribunal Members or legal representatives doing this. It can help to clarify what grounds are being relied on and what is not disputed by the patient. For example, if you look again at the case example of 'Mr D' above, it might look something like this:*

  MD – ✓

  N – ✓

  D – X

  H – ✓

  S – X

  P – ✓

  AMT – ✓

  (Continued)

Here, the RC thinks Mr D has a mental disorder that is of a nature but not of a degree to make it appropriate for him to be liable to be detained. The RC thinks detention is necessary for the interests of Mr D's health and for the protection of others but is not concerned about his safety. The RC is of the view that appropriate medical treatment is available at the hospital where Mr D is detained.

- *Remember your 'and's and 'or's – these are important terms in statutes. So, 'nature or degree', for example, means you do not necessarily have to make the case for both – one will suffice.*

- *Insight is not in the legal criteria. Be prepared to explain what you mean by this and how it might relate to the patient's capacity on a specific issue.*

Chapter summary

- There are legal criteria that are applicable to almost every case: mental disorder, nature or degree, health or safety or the protection of others.

- These criteria largely mirror the admission criteria, which professionals will probably be more familiar with.

- Much of the evidence and questioning in most hearings will be related to these criteria.

- There are sometimes subtle differences in the criteria for each section.

- The 'burden' remains on the patient to satisfy the Tribunal that the criteria are no longer met in Guardianship and conditionally discharged restricted patient cases.

Chapter 7
Preparing written evidence

Introduction

This chapter refers to the legal requirements for Tribunal reports in both England and Wales as set out in the relevant Practice Directions. We provide some introductory points which are relevant to all professional reports for the Tribunal, general advice and tips on preparing written evidence and explain the specific rules on withholding information.

There are some additional points on facilities reports and the NHS England Transforming Care Agenda for those with learning disabilities and/or autism spectrum disorders.

The subsequent sub-chapters will go on to consider the specific requirements in the Practice Direction (PD) for the Responsible Clinician (RC), nursing and social circumstances reports, including additional requirements for under 18s.

The Practice Direction

Practice Directions (PDs) are supplementary detailed procedural guidance to the Tribunal Rules. For the purposes of this book, we are referring only to the PDs for writing professional reports. The English and Welsh PDs are slightly different and where necessary we will make this clear to the reader. Compliance with the PD is required by the Rules and a failure by a party to comply with the Rules or the PD could give rise to a number of actions by the Tribunal, for example, to compel a document to be produced or to compel a person to attend and to give evidence.

The PDs for England and Wales can be found at:

www.judiciary.uk/wp-content/uploads/JCO/Documents/Practice+Directions/ Tribunals/statements-in-mental-health-cases-hesc-28102013.pdf

And:

https://mentalhealthreviewTribunal.gov.wales/sites/mentalhealthreview/files/2019- 12/MHRT%20Practice%20Direction%20Oct%202019.pdf

There are editable templates for reports available at:

www.gov.uk/government/collections/mental-health-Tribunal-forms

However, there is no requirement to use these versions.

We are aware that many professionals do not follow the headings in the relevant PD. Some may not be aware of them and others prefer to write in their own style. If the report is set out logically and covers the necessary information, that is what matters, but it is likely that, at a hearing, you may be asked about issues if they are in the PD headings and you have failed to cover them in your report. We have heard criticism that the PD may constrain professionals to only address the required headings, risking important information being omitted from reports where the author does not feel it fits into any specific heading.

Both the English and Welsh PD are set out in categories and paragraphs, for example, inpatient reports are at 'Category A' and the RC report requirements for inpatients are at 'Para 12a'.

Statement of information

The PDs require a 'Statement of Information' about the patient from the Responsible Authority, sometimes referred to as the 'Part A Statement'. You will find this at the start of each category. This information is usually collated by the Mental Health Act Administration in the relevant hospital or Local Authority if a Guardianship patient. Most of the headings in the PDs are self-explanatory, requiring information such as the first language of the patient and any requirements for a British Sign Language signer or interpreter; a list of previous admissions, discharges, renewals, Community Treatment Orders (CTOs), recalls and extensions; the names of the patient's RC, Care Coordinator and, where relevant, private Guardian; the responsible NHS and Local Authority for s.117 aftercare funding purposes; the details of the patient's Nearest Relative (NR) and any representative; details of any legal proceedings relating to the patient's mental capacity or ability to handle their own affairs.

Along with this statement of information, the necessary professional reports have to be collated and filed with the Tribunal within the relevant time frames (see Chapter 8).

The importance of timely filing of reports is emphasised in the English and Welsh Codes of Practice (12.12 (E) and 12.14(W)):

> *Missing, out-of-date or inadequate reports can lead to adjournments or unnecessarily long hearings. Where RCs, social workers, or other professionals are required to provide reports, they should do this promptly and within the statutory timescale.*

There are two paragraphs of the PDs that require further explanation:

First, the requirements in the statement of information include details of the responsible authorities for s.117 aftercare. This should include the relevant NHS body and Local Authority. Not all patients are eligible for s.117 aftercare, but it should be clear when they are and which bodies are responsible for providing it. If there are any disputes as to which body is responsible, that should be noted.

Second, the statement of information also asks for details of the patient's NR or the person exercising that function. Although the English and Welsh PD vary slightly in the information required, both require the relevant details where known, of who the NR is, and whether or not the patient has requested that their NR should *not* be informed of their treatment and care or consulted about their views for the Tribunal proceedings. The additional requirement is to state whether or not in the view of the Responsible Authority the patient has the capacity to make such a request. It is our experience that MHA Administrators who usually supply this information will rely on nursing staff's assessment of any capacity issues.

The Practice Direction: General guidance for all reports

What is the purpose of the written evidence?

Both PDs (England and Wales) state in their introductions that the Tribunal Rules require certain statements and reports to be submitted to the Tribunal. Both PDs specify the details required in these reports. In Chapter 1 we looked at the 'burden of proof' and the fact that in most cases the burden lies with the Responsible Authority. Professionals need to be mindful that the reports are the written evidence on the Responsible Authority's position as to why the patient still needs to be subject to the MHA. The clinical and social reports provide the 'backbone of this evidence' (MHA Code 12.4 (E), 12.3 (W)).

However, this need not mean that the relevant authors of, for example, the inpatient nursing report or social circumstances report must necessarily agree with the position of the RC and we shall look at this later. A well-argued, cohesive report following the requirements of the PD is much more helpful to the Tribunal (and to the patient) than one with gaps, contradictions and lacking evidence for professional opinion. Remember that the evidence will be further tested during the hearing and a report with omissions, inconsistencies or a lack of referencing of sources is likely to open the door to more rigorous questioning by the Panel and cross-examination by the legal representative.

> ### *EXPERT QUOTE*
>
> *Preparation is key. Be familiar with your report. If you did not write it, be familiar with it and make your own decision as to whether you agree with it or have a different opinion – you are the person who will be giving evidence at the hearing.*

Who sees my report?

The Tribunal Rules specify who has sight of the reports. Your report will be seen by the Panel, the patient, their representative, any other professionals attending to give evidence and any expert witnesses who have been instructed. See below for details in relation to the with-holding of information from the patient.

Should the report reflect my own personal professional views or those of an organisation?

You should not be asked to vary or amend a report to reflect someone else's position. If you need to explain the position from a managerial perspective or that of other agencies, then say so. If your department has a particular policy on something (e.g. discharge planning), then clarify this. This can be separate from your own professional judgement, which should be your own opinion in light of the facts and evidence available to you. It should go without saying that reports must honestly reflect the author's professional opinion – all professional witnesses have a duty under the Rules to assist the Tribunal to deal with the case fairly and justly. As we have established, the Tribunal is a Court and therefore misleading the Tribunal risks being deemed a contempt of Court.

On occasions when the author is unable to attend the hearing and someone else attends in their place they will be asked if they have read and agree with the contents of the report and explain any difference of opinion or updating information.

EXPERT QUOTE

Your written evidence is your primary evidence, and the Tribunal will accept this as your substantive evidence. If things have changed since the time the report was written, you will be invited to give an update; do not be afraid of changing what you have written; if the facts have changed, then it follows that the conclusion must also have changed, even if only to some small degree.

Read and spell check your reports. A report full of spelling and grammatical errors gives a very poor impression of the report writer. It suggests a lack of care and commitment.

What are the Practice Direction requirements for reports?

Responsible Authorities and authors of reports should refer to the relevant part of the PD when preparing their written reports as this sets out the categories and the information required from each professional, as follows:

CATEGORY A	Inpatients (non-restricted and restricted) – see next paragraph for a definition of inpatient for these purposes.
CATEGORY B	Community patients (patients subject to a Community Treatment Order s.17A)
CATEGORY C	Guardianship patients
CATEGORY D	Conditionally discharged patients
CATEGORY E	Patients under the age of 18 (applies to the social circumstances report only)

Figure 7.1   Practice Direction by category of patient

Each category then requires a statement of information (as described above) before listing the requirements for individual professional reports as follows:

- RC's report;

- Inpatient nursing report (and there are some additional requirements in the Welsh PD for nursing reports in other cases);

- Social circumstances report (SCR) (and additional requirements in the Welsh PD for SCR reports to reflect the requirements of the Mental Health (Wales) Measure 2010).

Inpatients (non-Restricted and restricted)

Both the Welsh and English Practice Directions explain in the introduction that:

For the purposes of this Practice Direction, a patient is an in-patient if they are detained in hospital to be assessed or treated for a mental disorder, whether admitted through civil or criminal justice processes, including a restricted patient (i.e. subject to special restrictions under the Act.) and including a patient transferred to hospital from custody. A patient is to be regarded as an in-patient detained in a hospital even if they have been permitted leave of absence or have gone absent without leave.

General PD requirements for all reports

The English and Welsh PD require that:

The authors of reports should have personally met and be familiar with the patient. If an existing report becomes out-of-date, or the status or circumstances of the patient change after the reports have been written but before the Tribunal takes place (e.g. if a patient is discharged or is recalled), the author of the report should then send it to the Tribunal an addendum addressing the up-to-date situation and, where necessary, the new applicable statutory criteria.

For each professional and in each case all reports must be:

up-to-date, specifically prepared for the Tribunal and have numbered paragraphs and pages. Reports should be signed and dated. The sources for information for the events and incidents described must be clear. Reports should not recite details of medical records or be an addendum to (or reproduce extensive details from) previous reports …

Both the Welsh and English PD require that *all* reports include the following:

Whether there are any factors that might affect the patient's understanding or ability to cope with a hearing and whether there are any adjustments that the Tribunal may consider in order to deal with the case fairly and justly.

- The SCR in all cases should include details of any Care Pathway [sic] Approach (CPA) and/or s.117 aftercare plan in full or in embryo (England) and for Wales the Care Coordinator should provide information set out in s.18 of the Mental Health (Wales) Measure 2010 including an up-to-date Care and Treatment Plan. For under 18s this includes a specific requirement to state which public bodies either have worked together or need to liaise in relation to aftercare services under s.117 MHA. See below for more details on the PD requirements for under 18s.

- The *'strengths and positive factors relating to the patient'*. For the patient, having to sit and listen to reports on one's presentation and life circumstances, particularly in situations where a patient might not agree, can be upsetting and frustrating. Inevitably, if professionals are making the case for continued detention the reports will contain information which the patient is likely to perceive as negative or critical. Strengths and positive factors are an important balance and should be broader than the treatment plan and the patient's mental health.

- The patient's views, wishes, beliefs, opinions, hopes and concerns are required in all SCRs.

- All reports ask for any recommendations to the Tribunal with reasons. You do not have to agree with your colleagues. Differences of opinion are inevitable at times. It is, however, always preferable to have identified and discussed any differing views ahead of giving evidence to the Tribunal. It is also one of many very good reasons for reading the other professionals' reports when preparing for a hearing as differences of opinion are very likely to be questioned by the Panel or the legal representative. Professionals should not be asked whether they would sign a medical recommendation or application for detention now. As discussed in Chapter 6, the Courts have recognised that a patient seeking discharge from hospital is in a very different position to a person being assessed for admission in the first place. The Panel will understand if the author of a report is unfamiliar with the patient and does not feel able to give a recommendation.

FAQ: I have been asked to write the report on someone I don't know. What should I do?

Answer: It is important to clarify why it is not possible for someone who does know the patient to write the relevant report. However, it might be that this is their first admission and they are unknown to services.

In relation to the SCR, it is likely in some areas that this might be written by a Local Authority employee who is not connected with the relevant NHS body.

In these cases, it is worth being clear to the Panel what your professional background is, who you are employed by, and being clear in the introduction how long you have known the patient and in what capacity.

If you do not know the patient, then liaise with those who do. Ensure that you take information from a range of sources and evidence this. Follow the relevant PD headings and explain to the Tribunal all you have done and your knowledge (even if limited) of the patient's case.

If it is at all possible to meet the patient ahead of the hearing, even briefly, you should do so. If not, at least attempt to speak with the patient over the phone. Your report should be shared with the patient and it should reflect their own views and opinions as well as yours.

A legal representative is almost certainly going to provide copies to the patient or at least discuss the contents with them anyway and it is probably more helpful to the patient to be able to discuss the report contents with the author who may be able to put information into context. If it has not been possible to meet with the patient or share your report, explain why in the introduction.

Don't forget to also try and read the other reports so that you are aware of the views of the other professionals.

Danger to self or others?

For almost all reports, the Practice Direction (both England and Wales) require professionals to give an opinion on:

whether the patient, if discharged from hospital, would be likely to act in a manner dangerous to themselves or others.

This legal test is only applicable when a NR order for discharge has been barred and they have made their own application to the Tribunal. It is therefore only relevant for such a Tribunal and not applicable in any others. Curiously (and in our view mistakenly), this heading appears in almost every report requirement without any qualification and therefore authors understandably try to complete it. See Chapter 6 for more details on the legal criteria for each case and how the law is applied in Tribunals.

Meaning of index offence/forensic history

All RC and SCR reports in all categories of patients require details of any index offence(s) and other relevant forensic history. Our experience has been that this is often misunderstood in reports. 'Forensic' in this context simply means 'from the Courts' and this section should really only include matters such as convictions, charges, cautions and any other criminal proceedings. Incidents on the ward, for example, might be relevant to the case but should be included elsewhere in the report if they did not lead to any criminal procedure. 'Index offence' is the offence (or most serious of several offences) that led to the patient being detained in hospital *on this occasion* by way of a Court order or prison transfer.

This is a section of the reports where it is particularly important to reference your sources, ideally from the patient's formal record of previous convictions if available.

Lacking capacity and the eligible compliant patient

The English Practice Direction include the following headings for *all* inpatient RC and SCR reports and the Welsh Practice Direction has the same subheading for SCR reports for inpatients at Section 14 of the PD:

> *In the case of an eligible compliant patient who lacks capacity to agree or object to their detention or treatment, whether or not deprivation of liberty under the Mental Capacity Act 2005 (as amended) would be appropriate and less restrictive.*

This was added following the Upper Tribunal case of *AM v South London and Maudsley NHS Foundation Trust* [2013]. In short, does the patient lack capacity to make a decision regarding admission and any assessment/treatment at the psychiatric hospital? If so, are they compliant and likely to remain compliant for the foreseeable future with the admission and any assessment/treatment there? Is it likely that the admission will amount to a deprivation of liberty? In these cases, might the Deprivation of Liberty Safeguards (DoLS) be a less restrictive option?

Further information on this case and the practical considerations can be found in both the English and Welsh MHA Codes in Chapter 13. It is likely that similar questions will continue to apply when the Liberty Protection Safeguards are in force.

Deprivation of liberty in the community

It will be relevant to include any details where the relevant patient (CTO, Guardianship, conditionally discharged) is also subject to a Court authorisation or DoLS authorisation depriving them of their liberty in the community or the plan is for this to be applied for in advance of any such discharge (see Chapter 6).

Introductory information in all professional reports

We suggest that all reports should start by:

- identifying the author, their professional role and what part they play in the patient's care (Care Coordinator, key-nurse, RC or other);
- how long they have known the patient in this capacity;
- what information they took account of in the writing of their report. For example, interview with the patient, electronic notes, discussion with RC, attendance at Care Programme Approach (CPA) or ward reviews, etc.

Even when this might be in the statement of information provided by the Responsible Authority, this information should also be at the head of your report so that it is accessible to the Tribunal Panel.

Safeguarding concerns

We also suggest that, although the PDs do not specifically request this information, that professionals should explain any previous or active safeguarding concerns, steps taken under the Care Act 2014 or Social Services and Wellbeing (Wales) Act 2014 in response to this and if not, why not. The reason and the current status of any concerns should be provided.

Additional reports

Facilities reports

These reports are not a requirement within the Practice Direction. They are usually provided in addition to the SCR for patients in out of area placements when an on-site professional writes the SCR and the home authority provide additional information on the local facilities available on discharge.

The information that proves most useful is that which contributes towards the subheadings in the SCR report for the relevant patient. This will often be around discharge plans, support on discharge and any funding issues.

A facilities report that simply details all of the services available in the local community, e.g. local sports centres, libraries, Citizens Advice Bureaus etc., is of little or no use and the reports should be tailored to the individual patient.

Care and Treatment Reviews and Care and Treatment Plans (England)

The Transforming Care agenda in England aims to reduce the admission to mental health hospitals of people with learning disabilities and/or autism spectrum disorders. Part of this agenda includes the development of Care and Treatment Reviews, described as follows:

> *Care and Treatment Reviews (CTRs) are part of NHS England's commitment to trans-forming services for people with learning disabilities, autism or both. CTRs are for people whose behaviour is seen as challenging and/or for people with a mental health condition. They are used by commissioners for people living in the community and in learning disability and mental health hospitals.*

> *(see www.england.nhs.uk/learning-disabilities/care/ctr/)*

CTRs should lead to adults having a Care and Treatment Plan (CTPs) or Care, Treatment and Education Plan (CTEP) for those under 18. These should be made available to the Tribunal in addition to the relevant reports.

NHS England guidance (Care and Treatment Review: Policy and Guidance, 2015, p38) sets out how the CTRs and CTPs assist the Tribunal:

> *The effectiveness of a Tribunal depends on the information that is available or presented to Tribunal Members and through the patient's legal representative. The views and wishes of Nearest Relatives will also need to be taken into account. CTRs have an important role to play in improving the quality and quantity of information and the quality of care and treatment plans that will come before a Tribunal.*

There is already a duty under Part 2 of the Mental Health (Wales) Measure 2010 for all detained patients, CTO and Guardianship patients and some informal patients to have a Care and Treatment Plan, not to be confused with the CTR above.

Withholding information

When professionals are concerned about information in their reports being disclosed to the patient or to any other person, the Rules (14(3) (E), 17(2) (W)) provide the Tribunal with the power to withhold the information in limited circumstances.

The Rules set out that if 'the first party' considers that the Tribunal should give a direction … prohibiting the disclosure of part or all of a document or information to another party, they must provide the relevant document or information to the Tribunal and the reason why it should be withheld. This allows the Tribunal to decide whether it should be disclosed to the second party or should be the subject of a direction specifying the limits or form of the disclosure.

The Courts and Tribunal Service: Reports for Mental Health Tribunals 2012 offers the following guidance:

> *If the Responsible Authority or the source or author of the information, statement, report or document considers that the Tribunal should give a direction prohibiting the disclosure of the material to the patient, they must*
>
> a. *separate and exclude the relevant information, statement, report or document from any other material submitted*
>
> b. *separately provide to the Tribunal copies of the excluded information, statement, report or document, ensuring that the excluded material is clearly marked: NOT TO BE DISCLOSED TO THE PATIENT WITHOUT THE EXPRESS PERMISSION OF THE TRIBUNAL*
>
> c. *provide the Tribunal will full written reasons for the proposed exclusion so that the Tribunal may decide for itself whether the grounds for exclusion have been made out and whether the information, statement, report or document should be disclosed to the patient, or whether it should be excluded.*

In practice, this issue only arises in relation to information being disclosed to or withheld from the patient. We saw in Chapter 1 the importance of the Article 6 ECHR right to a fair hearing. The Courts have set the bar for withholding information from a patient very high and, as far as the Rules are concerned, information will only be withheld if:

a. *disclosure would be likely to cause any person 'serious harm' and*

b. *it is in the interests of justice and proportionate to withhold the information.*

The Rules do not define 'serious harm' but the case-law gives an indication:

> ### CASE STUDY
>
> **RM v St Andrew's Healthcare *[2010] UKUT 119 (AAC)***
>
> *The patient suffered from organic delusional and personality disorders as well as epilepsy. In an earlier Tribunal, the patient had been informed that he had been covertly medicated. In response, the patient became very suspicious of eating and drinking, and consequently there was a serious deterioration in his physical and mental health, leading to restraint, seclusion and a concern about sudden death.*
>
> *The covert medication was reinstated and in the course of the next Tribunal proceedings, the Responsible Authority sought to withhold two addendum reports which revealed the covert treatment due to concerns about the same physical and mental health concerns arising again. The Tribunal initially agreed to withhold the reports from the patient and this decision was appealed.*
>
> *Despite the risks, the Upper Tribunal upheld the appeal, ordered disclosure of the reports to the patient and said:*
>
> *The Convention right under Article 6 guarantees a fair hearing.*
>
> - 'The overriding objective in Rule 2 requires … that cases are dealt with fairly and justly. This includes ensuring full participation, so far as practicable … Justice and fairness generally require openness'.
> - Withholding the reports 'would exclude the claimant completely from knowing of the real process that was being followed and allow him to participate only in a pretence of a process. They would severely hamper his legal team in participating effectively in that process'.

The effect of the Rules, Article 6 ECHR and the relevant case-law mean that it would be very unwise to give any assurances to a relative or other person that information they provide for the purposes of a report being completed will not be disclosed to the patient. It is entirely a decision for the Tribunal. If you are considering asking for information not to be disclosed, then we would also suggest that you check whether the information has been disclosed elsewhere in other reports, for example. It is also worth considering carefully how essential the information is to the case – if the information is not relevant to the criteria for detention or the PD headings, then there may be nothing to be gained by including it in your report and dilemmas about withholding the information could be avoided.

As well as the 'serious harm' test, there may also be complex situations involving information that is confidential to a third party and therefore there is a conflict between the patient's right to a fair hearing and the third party's right to privacy. The Upper Tribunal has said that hospitals and legal representatives should seek to resolve these matters by agreement (for example, by exchanging written arguments) ahead of the hearing where possible, but an application to the Tribunal for a direction can still be made if no resolution can be reached (*Dorset Healthcare NHS Foundation Trust v MH* [2009]).

Tips and guidance on writing reports for the Tribunal

Reports usually integrate a range of fact and opinion. They may include information from other sources (third party or hearsay); hearsay being a fact or opinion from someone other than the person giving evidence. The Tribunal will decide what weight to give a particular piece of information, but as a general rule hearsay evidence will be treated more cautiously and the longer the 'chain' of hearsay the less reliable it will be felt to be. For example, A told me that B had told him that he had heard from C, etc.

> *If the Tribunal is relying on hearsay evidence it must take into account the fact that it is hearsay and must have regard to the particular dangers involved in relying upon second, third or fourth hand hearsay. The Tribunal must be appropriately cautious of relying upon assertions as to past events which are not securely recorded in contemporaneous notes, particularly if the only evidence is hearsay.*
>
> (R(on the application of AN) v MHRT *[2005]*)

Facts

Both the English and Welsh PDs require that for all reports: 'all sources of information for the events and incidents described must be made clear'. As we saw in Chapter 1, the Tribunal applies the civil standard of proof and will assess matters on the 'balance of probabilities' – i.e. is something more likely than not to have happened. That said, case-law has established that there is some flexibility in how this standard can be applied. In particular, it is important to be aware that the more serious the allegation, or consequences for the patient if the allegation is found to be true, the better the quality of evidence that will be expected to be provided in support of it.

Information being presented as factual should be referenced if possible, any limitations on the veracity of the information acknowledged and the patient's views about the information made clear if it is contentious.

Descriptive accounts with no summary

It is worth carefully considering what you are writing and why you want the Tribunal Panel, other professionals and the patient to read it. Listing long details from nursing or clinical notes is unhelpful unless there is a clear purpose for including the information. It is a general requirement of the PDs that reports should not recite medical records or reproduce extensive details from previous reports.

For example, here is an anonymised extract from an inpatient nursing report for a patient detained on s.3:

1st March	*Agitated, verbally abusive to staff.*
2nd March	*Irritable and aggressive towards staff.*
3rd March	*Leave refused – agitated and abusive.*
4th March	*Agitated and irritable toward staff. Called Staff Nurse X 'a bitch' for refusing leave.*

This extract was several pages long with similar entries to those above and you can see that it would be of no use to a Tribunal trying to address the statutory criteria or evaluate risks. This is usually referred to as a descriptive account with no analysis. There is no point in listing pages of entries directly from nursing notes unless the author is prepared to formulate a summary based on their own professional judgement and opinion. Listing information indiscriminately does not evidence understanding of its relevance and can affect the credibility of the author.

It would be far more helpful, therefore, for the author to simply note that in the month of March, there were daily entries of agitated and aggressive behaviour (including exactly what and to whom) and any triggers or reasons for the incidents.

A Tribunal Panel is likely to ask the author what its relevance is rather than guess at what the author might have meant.

Cutting and pasting information

Cutting and pasting information from previous reports can lead to problems if it is not possible to verify the information or its origins. Sources for cut and pasted information should always be cited. Failing to do this may lead to:

> *The well-known problem that constant repetition in 'official' reports or statements may, in the 'official' mind, turn into established fact something which rigorous forensic investigation shows is in truth nothing more than 'institutional folk lore' with no secure foundation in either recorded or provable fact.*

> (R(on the application of AN) v MHRT *[2005]*)

EXPERT QUOTE

Avoid cutting and pasting huge swathes of past reports or notes. Report writing is a filtration exercise bringing together the threads of a number of documents and conversations. Long reports do not make good reports.

Some reports particularly on forensic cases are over 40 pages long and include reams of copy and pasted material going back over many years. This makes it very difficult for the Panel to see the wood from the trees. In these cases a brief report probably takes more time to prepare but is a far more useful document. Cutting and pasting causes some awful mistakes in reports. Changes in font and letter size are giveaways.

All Tribunal reports require a chronology listing the patient's previous involvement with mental health services, including admissions, discharges, any recalls etc. Patients will often state that reports are inaccurate when detailing history, past behaviour or events. In some instances, where professionals have relied on previous reports they cannot always tell the Tribunal where the evidence originated. In these cases, it is worth being honest and documenting this in the report.

In addition, where templates or electronic notes require professionals to complete risk assessments, an explanation and rationale for reaching a professional judgement is required.

ACTIVITY **7.2**

Read the two extracts below from real Tribunal reports, and note down your thoughts on each question.

Inpatient nursing report

RISK BEHAVIOUR	LOW	MEDIUM	HIGH
Physical aggression	√		

Question:

- *What questions might the Tribunal Panel ask the inpatient nurse who attends the hearing?*
  - ○ *More details of the event that led to an assessment of low risk of physical aggression.*
  - ○ *Whether the patient has ever been a medium or high risk of physical aggression.*
  - ○ *What events led to this risk assessment?*
  - ○ *How was the risk reduced to low?*
  - ○ *Who was at risk from any physical aggression?*

In the extract above, it transpired that the patient had no history of physical aggression. However, when questioned, the nurse was able to report that the inpatient risk assessment template did not have 'None' in the options.

Question:

- *How might an inpatient nurse better deal with this when writing their report?*

ACTIVITY **7.3**

Read the extract below and consider what questions are likely to arise at the Tribunal for the author of the SCR?

RC report:	SCR:
His Mother reports that prior to the last admission, he had received some information on psychosis from his Care Coordinator. This was his first episode of psychosis and he was understandably upset. He sat at the kitchen table and set fire to this document in an ashtray. He quickly doused the flames and his Mother was present.	Apparently he set a small fire in his Mother's house recently.

Factual information incorporating the views of the patient

It is important to acknowledge when a patient disputes a factual matter in a report, not least because it will make going through the report with the patient a much easier and potentially more positive process. For example:

In 1998 the psychiatric records note that Alex assaulted a neighbour. However, they do not clarify whether police were involved and Alex has consistently stated that this is not accurate information. In Alex's view, the neighbour instigated an assault following an argument on the pavement. This led to the admission to hospital in 1998. There is no mention of this event in social services or police records.

Professional opinion

Statements that express a view or belief are opinions. These are valid but need to be clearly set out as opinions, e.g. I think, I believe, I consider, it is my opinion.

Professionals give expert opinion within their area of expertise. Professional opinion that makes logical links to facts, history and knowledge of the case is helpful. Expert professional opinion is difficult to challenge if rationally presented. For example:

It is my professional opinion that Ms Y continues to suffer from a delusional disorder. This is based on the continuing symptoms she suffers from and are referred to in my report, research evidence from the diagnostic manual and relevant historical information from family, her GP and previous treating team.

Or:

It is my professional opinion that Mr X could not yet cope with independent living. This is based on the OT assessment of his daily living skills attached, the recent psychological assessment of his current functioning confirming that he is as yet unable to identify how he would manage various aspects of daily living, my own assessment on 1 February 2020 and 3 April 2020 and in liaison with his wife and father on 3 April 2020, a report from his GP and a Care Act assessment completed on 5 April 2020.

Opinion Without Evidence

Here are some real examples from Tribunal reports:

- *The nursing team does not feel that John is ready for discharge.*

- *He lacks insight.*

- *She does not engage.*

- *She is unlikely to ever manage in an independent living situation.*

- *He requires 24-hour care.*

You should be prepared for further questions from the Tribunal Panel and the legal representative about statements like these that are not supported with evidence.

> ### *EXPERT QUOTE*
>
> *Hospital reports often leave out vital information about prior periods outside hospital even if they were very lengthy. Details of previous treatment and after-care may be very important in assessing future need.*

Top tips

- *Follow the Practice Direction. It would be difficult for anyone to be critical of your report if this is done properly.*

- *Ask yourself why you are including any nursing and medical notes (e.g. pages and pages of observations) and what exactly it is you are trying to evidence – can it be done any more succinctly?*

- *Be wary of cutting and pasting information from other documents and cite your sources if you do.*

- *Think carefully about non-disclosure issues and how you intend to show the grounds for non-disclosure are met. You cannot make any promises to third parties that something will not be disclosed – it will be a decision for the Tribunal.*

- *Share and go through your report with the patient ahead of the hearing.*

- *Acknowledge if information is not substantiated and check for inconsistencies in your own report or with other reports.*

- *Positive evidence about the patient is important.*

- *You are allowed to 'not know'.*

- *You are not obliged to agree with other professionals or their reports. However, where you do disagree, it is best to try and discuss these issues ahead of the Tribunal and at least be fully informed on each other's point of view. Read your colleague's reports.*

- *Preserve your relationship with your client. Acknowledge differences of opinion: I know Ms X disagrees with me about this but …*

- *Keep a logical link between facts and opinion or recommendations.*

Chapter summary

- The English and Welsh Practice Directions provide detailed requirements for the contents of the professional reports being submitted in Tribunal proceedings for every category of patient subject to the MHA.

- Some requirements of the Practice Directions such as those dealing with the statutory criteria are common to all categories, but some categories of patients have specific requirements that need to be dealt with. It is essential to follow the correct template for a particular patient.

- Reports for under 18s have some complex requirements that require at least a working knowledge of other legal frameworks to complete properly (or at least access to a professional colleague who might be able to assist).

Responsible Clinician's reports

Responsible Clinician's reports: General points

As we saw earlier in this chapter, the relevant headings for reports are within the Practice Direction (PD). Although England and Wales have separate PDs setting out the required headings for reports, there is much overlap. The PD for Wales includes an Appendix which incorporates the relevant Rules, Schedule 1 and includes Part A, B, C and D additional requirements for all cases.

In the grids below you will see a reference to the relevant category of patient, the paragraphs dealing with the specific reports and any differences between England and Wales. We do not refer to any paragraphs that are self-explanatory and focus on the paragraphs that require some additional analysis. Further information on the statutory criteria and relevant legal issues, such as those regarding learning disability, is in Chapter 6 ('How do Tribunals apply the law?').

There are some generic points:

- All Responsible Clinician's (RC) reports should be written by the RC or counter signed by the RC when written by another clinician.

- Note that the PD for England requires an explanation in all inpatient, Community Treatment Order (CTO) and Guardianship cases whether the patient has a learning disability and if so, whether that disability is associated with abnormally aggressive or seriously irresponsible conduct.

- The PD for Wales requires that, if the patient is under 18 and the RC is not a Child and Adolescent Mental Health Services (CAMHS) specialist, they will need to ensure a report from such a specialist is provided to the Tribunal.

- The PD for England and Wales requires a detailed chronology in all cases, listing the patient's previous involvement with mental health services, any admissions, discharges, or previous CTOs or Guardianship, etc. It is particularly helpful to also refer back to any periods where the patient was not admitted and how they managed whilst in the community.

Responsible Clinician's report – inpatients (Category A Para 12 (England and Wales))

Paragraph	Key points
England Paras (f), (h) and (i).	The England and Wales PDs have some separate requirements for inpatients.
Para (f)	For further details on the statutory criteria see Chapter 6.
Whether the patient is now suffering from a mental disorder and, if so, whether a diagnosis has been made, what the diagnosis is, and why.	
Para (h)	
Depending upon the statutory criteria, whether any mental disorder present is of a nature or degree to warrant or make appropriate, liability to be detained in a hospital for assessment and/or medical treatment.	
Para (i)	
Details of any appropriate and available medical treatment prescribed, provided, offered or planned for the patient's mental disorder.	

Wales Appendix, Schedule 1,	
Part B, Para 1	
An up-to-date clinical report … including the relevant clinical history and a full report of the patient's mental condition.	

Responsible Clinician's report – community patients (Category B Para 18 England and Wales)

The introduction to Para 18 in the PD for Wales states what the report must include, so far as it is applicable the information set out above in relation to inpatients. Hence, you will see in the boxes below references to Para 12. The PD for England set out headings from Para 18 (a)–(u) and do not refer back to the inpatient reports.

Paragraph	Key points
Para (a) *Where the patient is aged 18 or over and the case is a reference to the Tribunal, whether the patient has capacity to decide whether or not to attend or be represented at a Tribunal hearing.*	This paragraph is specifically in relation to references to the Tribunal, where the patient has not applied. Patients on CTOs are, of course, in the community and it is not unusual for patients to lose interest in Tribunal proceedings once they are out of hospital. This additional question will assist the Tribunal to decide whether the patient has made a capacitous decision to not attend or be represented. If the CTO Tribunal hearing arises from a reference, then it is open to the patient to request a 'paper review' in England but not in Wales (see Chapter 4).
England Para (h) and Wales Para (c) *The conditions to which the patient was made subject under Section 17B when the CTO was put in place and details of any variation of those conditions since then.*	List the CTO conditions here. Following on from this, any details of and reasons for variation to the original *discretionary* conditions.
England Para (h) and Wales Para (d) *Details of the patients compliance with the conditions imposed under s17B together with details of any recalls to hospital under s17E which have not resulted in a revocation of the CTO.*	How well have the conditions worked? Has the patient adhered to the mandatory *and* discretionary conditions? The PD in Wales also requires the RC to specify any incidences where a recall has *not* led to the revocation of the CTO and why not.
England Para 18(e) and Wales Para 12 (d) *Reasons for any previous admission or recall to hospital.*	As well as setting out details of the circumstances leading up to admission, whether the CTO recall power has been used and if so, the outcome of the recall on each occasion. In addition, whether the patient has been admitted informally without the requirement of recall.

(Continued)

(Continued)

Paragraph	Key points
England Para (t) *Whether it continues to be necessary that the Responsible Clinician should be able to exercise the power of recall and, if so, why.* The PD for Wales requires the author of the social circumstances report at Para 19(e), to complete this paragraph.	The RC is required to explain why they believe it continues to be necessary that they should be able to exercise the power of recall and if so, why. This is a key part of the statutory criteria, and will form part of the questioning of the RC. In many CTO cases this is the criterion that tends to be questioned the most. Why is recall 'necessary' rather than 'desirable'? Where a patient has not been recalled for a lengthy period of time, the report should set out how their care is managed in the community.

Responsible Clinician's report – Guardianship patients (Category C Para 23 England and Wales PD)

The PD for Wales defines a Guardianship patient for these purposes as a patient who has been received into Guardianship in accordance with s.7 of the Act.

The PD for England does not define this and one assumes therefore that those who are received into Guardianship as a result of a Court order under s.37 MHA are included. However, there are some key differences between s.7 and s.37 both in the initial criteria and in the powers of the Nearest Relative (see Chapter 6).

Note, once again that the introduction to Para 18 in the PD for Wales states that the report must include, so far as it is applicable the information set out above in relation to inpatients.

Paragraph	Key points
Para (e) *Any requirements to which the patient is subject under Section 8(1) and details of the patient's compliance.*	Is the patient required to reside at a specified place, attend at places and times for medical treatment, occupation, education or training, allow access to the patient to be given to any registered medical practitioner, AMHP or other person specified by the Guardian at any place they are residing. Note the power to impose requirements for s.37 Guardianship order patients are in s.40(2). Are there any issues with the requirements? If so, how these have been managed.

Paragraph	Key points
England Para (n) and Wales Para (j) *Whether it is necessary for the welfare of the patient, or for the protection of others, that the patient should remain under Guardianship and, if so, why.*	There is nothing in either the English or Welsh MHA Codes on the meaning of 'welfare'. However, we note that Jones (2020, p89) helpfully states the following in relation to s7(2)(b): *All factors which might affect the wellbeing of the patient are covered by this phrase, including the patient's need to be protected from exploitation. The wording is wide enough to encompass the need to prevent the patient's welfare from being prejudiced at some time in the future. If the concern relates to possible future harm, the recommending doctors would need to be satisfied that there is a real risk of such an eventuality occurring. E.g. an attempt by a relative to remove a mentally incompetent patient from a care setting to accommodation where the patient's welfare might be seriously prejudiced.*

Conditionally discharged patients

The PDs define a conditionally discharged patient as:

A conditionally discharged patient is a restricted patient who has been discharged from hospital into the community, subject to a condition that the patient will remain liable to be recalled to hospital for further treatment, should it become necessary.

When a conditionally discharged patient applies to the Tribunal, the Secretary of State must immediately provide the contact details for the Responsible Clinician and Social Supervisor to the Tribunal. The RC and Social Supervisor have three weeks to submit their reports from the time they are notified of the application. On receipt of the reports, the Secretary of State then has three weeks to submit to the Tribunal:

- A summary of the index offence;
- A record of any previous convictions;
- Details of the patient's liability to detention since the original restriction order was imposed;
- Any other information considered relevant;
- Any observations the Secretary of State wishes to make.

Both MHA Codes (12.13 (E), 12.17 (W)) state that in the case of a restricted patient, if the opinion of the RC or other professional providing the report changes from that which was recorded in the original Tribunal report this must be communicated in writing before the hearing to the relevant Tribunal Office and the Mental Health Unit of the Ministry of Justice (MoJ) enabling them to prepare a supplementary statement. A failure to do this might well give a ground of appeal to the Secretary of State or the Welsh Ministers should they oppose the outcome of the proceedings.

Practice Direction Category D Para 27 (E) and 28 (W) also states that:

> *Upon being notified by the Tribunal of an application or reference, the RC must send or deliver the RCs report and any Social Supervisor must send or deliver the social circumstances report (SCR). If there is no Social Supervisor, the Responsible Clinicians report should also provide the required social circumstances information.*

The RC may also send on any further report *'if in the opinion of the RC such reports are likely to help the Tribunal when they consider the matter'*.

The PD for Wales expressly sets out that the RC's report and SCR should address the criteria set out in paragraph 57 in *R(SC) v MHRT* [2005] (see Chapter 6). Although the PD for England does not refer directly to the 'SC' case, the relevant paragraphs set out below cover the salient points.

Responsible Clinician's report – conditionally discharged patients (Category D Para 32 England and Para 30 Wales)

Paragraph	Key points
Para 28 (Wales) *The RC and SCR reports should address the criteria as set out in the 'SC' case.* *Most of the criteria from this case are within the required paragraph headings, e.g. English Para 32 (q) (r) (s) (t) (u) and (v)* *Welsh Para 30 (m) (n) (o) (p) and (q)*	It would be sensible for RCs to deal with the 'SC' criteria expressly as Tribunals will usually treat them as quasi-statutory criteria. They are summarised below: *The Tribunal must consider such matters as the nature, gravity and circumstances of the patient's offence, the nature and gravity of the mental disorder, past present and future, the risk and likelihood of the patient re-offending, the degree of harm to which the public may be exposed if he re-offends, the risk and likelihood of a recurrence or exacerbation of any mental disorder, and the risk and likelihood of his needing to be recalled in the future for further treatment in hospital. The nature of any conditions previously imposed, reasons why and extent to which it is desirable to continue, vary or add to them.*

Paragraph	Key points
Para 32(g) and (h) (England); *Para 30(f) and (g) (Wales)* *Any conditions currently imposed (whether by the Tribunal or the Secretary of State) and the reasons why the conditions were imposed;* *details of the patient's compliance with any current conditions.*	The statement of information is not required to list the conditions. These should be clearly set out in the RCs report and easily accessible to the reader. The SCR is also required to list the conditions and compliance with these. Therefore, it will be important to liaise with each other to ensure any gaps or differences of opinion are highlighted.

Nursing reports

Nursing reports: General points

Nursing reports should be written by a nurse who is familiar with the patient and should detail their current nursing plan and the patients' current presentation. The Practice Direction (PD) for Wales requires the report to be written or countersigned by the patient's named nurse. The PD for England requires the patient's current nursing plan to be attached, although in our experience this is often forgotten.

Nursing report – inpatients (Category A Para 13 England and Wales)

The inpatient nursing report should give an account of the patient's day-to-day progress on the ward. Some of the headings simply require factual information on the current situation. Other headings ask for professional views. Overall, the report should give a clear picture of how things presently are for the patient on the ward.

The nursing team will usually be seeing the patient more often than the Responsible Clinician (RC) or author of the social circumstances report (SCR). It is important to have the courage of your convictions if you have any differing view from other professionals. Most nursing teams have an excellent grasp of the day-to-day progress and circumstances of the patient.

Paragraph	Key points
Para (b) *The nature of the nursing care and medication currently being made available; and*	List all medications. Any use of PRN (as required medication)? How often, when last used? Any physical health issues and relevant medication/investigations?

(Continued)

(Continued)

Paragraph	Key points
Para (c) *The level of observation to which the patient is currently subject.*	Has nursing care changed? Does the patient make use of protected time with the key-nurse? Do nurses have to prompt the patient with any aspects of their care? What level of observation is the patient subject to, and has this changed since initial admission? Does the patient currently have any s.17 leave and, if so, is this escorted or unescorted, how long is it for and how is it used?
Para (d) *Whether the patient has contact with relatives, friends or other patients, the nature of the interaction and what community support the patent has.*	In our experience this section is often missed off or has limited information within it. Nursing staff are most likely to be aware of any regular contact with family and friends. This can be key information in relation to support on discharge, and family are also likely to identify changes in presentation and progress. Nursing staff might be asked, for example, whether any contact with the ward and family has assisted with taking a collateral history of the patient's mental disorder.
Para (e) *Strengths and positive factors relating to the patient.*	See earlier in the chapter.
Para (f) *A summary of the patient's current progress, engagement with nursing staff, behaviour, co-operation, activities, self-care and insight.*	There is an overlap here with earlier headings, but as long as all the key areas are covered that is acceptable. If current progress appears delayed, explain why. Ensure that where any aspect of your report states that there is a limited engagement, staff can explain why they think that is and whether related to the nature or degree of the mental disorder or simply the patient's choice.
Para (g) *Any occasions where the patient has been absent without leave whilst leave liable to be detained, or occasions when the patient has failed to return as and when required after having been granted leave.*	Self-explanatory: listing any occasions where the patient has either gone absent without leave from the ward or failed to return from s.17 leave at the required time.

Paragraph	Key points
Para (h) *The patient's understanding of, compliance with, and likely future willingness to accept any prescribed medication or treatment for mental disorder that is or might be made available.*	Treatment includes the full range of treatments available such as medication, psychology, occupational therapy, psycho-social interventions etc. See earlier in the chapter for tips on how to ensure your views are backed up with facts and evidence.
Para (i) *Details of any incidents in hospital where the patient has harmed themselves or others, or threatened harm, or damaged property, or threatened damage.*	The PDs do not specify whether 'in hospital' means on this admission only. However, it is likely to be most helpful to focus on the current admission along with any significant historical incidents during previous admissions. Where the admission has been lengthy it should be clear when incidents last took place.
Para (j) *Any occasions on which the patient has been secluded or restrained, including the reasons why such seclusion or restraint was necessary.*	Self-explanatory: note that if this includes transfers between wards, explain the nature of the ward. Statements such as *'she was transferred from Butterfly ward back to Blackbird unit'* are meaningless to others unless they know more about the wards, e.g. acute to PICU, low to medium security, etc.
Para (k) *Whether (in Section 2 cases) detention in hospital, or (in all other cases), the provision of medical treatment in hospital, is justified or necessary in the interests of the patient's health or safety, or for the protection of others.*	In summary, can any of the assessment or treatment now take place outside of a ward environment or as an informal patient? Explain your professional judgement here and back it up with evidence. What is it about the patient's health or safety or safety of others that continue to make detention essential?
Para (l) *Whether the patient, if discharged from hospital, would be likely to act in a manner dangerous to themselves or others.*	As discussed in Chapter 6, 'dangerousness' is only part of the legal criteria in Nearest Relative (NR) 'barring order' cases.
Para (m) England only *Whether, and if so how, any risks could be managed effectively in the community, including the use of any lawful conditions or recall powers.*	Building on nursing staff's knowledge of the patient and how the patient has managed on any s.17 leave. How nursing staff (and the patient) have managed the risks. Nursing staff's professional judgement on whether the patient and community staff/family could manage the risks without the patient continuing to be detained.
England Para (n) and Wales Para (m) *Any recommendations to the Tribunal with reasons.*	Views and recommendations of the author or the nursing team as a whole following on from the paragraph above.

Nursing report – community patients (Category B Para 16 Wales only)

Paragraph	Key points
In addition to the reports required in accordance with Schedule 1 Part B to the Act the Responsible Authority must provide a nursing report in relation to all community patients. The nursing report should be written by the professional person with the main responsibility for supervising the patient's treatment in the community. In the event that neither the social circumstances report nor the nursing report are written by the patient's Care Coordinator giving full details of the performance of their functions under s.18 of the Mental Health (Wales) Measure 2010 together with the up-to-date Care and Treatment Plan for the patient.	The PDs do not set out any headings for these reports and we therefore suggest the author refers back to the relevant paragraphs in the inpatient nursing report along with the details opposite.

Nursing report – Guardianship patients (Category C Paras 21 and 25 Wales only)

Paragraph	Key points
Para 21 sets out the additional requirement for the Responsible Authority to provide a nursing report by the Managers of any residential facility in which the patient is required to live as a condition of the Guardianship Order.	This is referring to any specific requirement of residence in s.8(1)(a) MHA as detailed above in the RC reports (and although the PD does not refer to s.37 Guardianship Order patients, this can be found at s.40(2)). Given that the manager of any residential facility may not be a nurse, there may be a need to liaise with any nurses providing care to the patient in the residential facility.
Para 25 (a)–(h) *These paragraphs set out the headings for the reports required above.*	These are similar to the inpatient nursing report requirements, with the exception of Para (f), which requires the nursing report to set out whether the patient has absented themselves from the place they are required to reside. We would recommend adding any reasons and the context for the absence. As stated earlier in this chapter, it may be important to specify whether the patient is also subject to a DoLS authorisation or Court order authorising a deprivation of liberty at the residential establishment.

Social circumstances reports

Social circumstances reports (SCRs): General points

FAQ: Who should write the social circumstances report?

Answer: The case of AF v Nottinghamshire NHS Trust *[2015] has established that there is no legal requirement for this report to be written by a social worker or community nurse. Nor is there any legal requirement that this report and the inpatient nursing report must be written by different authors.*

Having said that, there are specific requirements in the Practice Direction (PD) for Wales for the Care Coordinator (see below).

Note that this chapter sets out the details of the PD for England and Wales. Wales also has an Appendix to the PD, including Schedule 1 and Parts A, B, C and D. In the grids below, you will see references to the relevant category of patient and the paragraphs that require further explanation.

These points are common to all SCRs:

- Category A Para 14 of the PD for Wales requires SCR reports for inpatients 'where possible' to be written or countersigned by the patient's Care Coordinator. Where the SCR is not written by the Care Coordinator, a separate report by the Care Coordinator should be provided giving the information set out in s.18 of the Mental Health (Wales) Measure 2010, including an up-to-date Care and Treatment Plan. In the case of Community Treatment Order (CTO) patients, where neither the SCR nor nursing report is written by the patient's Care Coordinator, the Responsible Authority should also provide a report by the Care Coordinator, giving full details of the performance of their functions under s.18 of the Mental Health (Wales) Measure 2010 together with the up-to-date Care and Treatment Plan for the patient.

- It is likely that the person best placed to complete the SCR is the Care Coordinator or equivalent if the patient is on a different care pathway. The Social Supervisor might be best placed to complete the SCR for a conditionally discharged patient.

The Nearest Relative (NR)

The relevant headings for all SCRs ask that, except in restricted cases (where the patient does not have an NR), the views of the NR are included unless, having consulted the patient, it would be inappropriate or impractical to consult the NR, in which case reasons for this view must be given and any attempts to rectify matters described.

Relatives and the NR are defined in s.26–s.28 of the Mental Health Act (MHA). The MHA Reference Guide 2015 gives helpful information on how to identify the NR. Suffice to say that the identification of the NR can change over time; it is not the same as the next of kin or a Lasting

Power of Attorney and, in some cases, the NR may have delegated their role to another or the Court may have appointed someone (including the Local Authority) to take on this role. In some cases, a patient may not have an NR or it may not have been possible to ascertain who it is.

The Approved Mental Health Professional (AMHP) and Hospital Managers have specific duties towards the NR and are therefore required to both identify them and inform/consult them at various points.

For the purposes of the PD, the relevant paragraphs require identification of the NR, a summary of their views or, if not contacted, the reasons why not. The PD refers to situations where it might be 'inappropriate' or 'impractical' to contact the NR for their views. This covers situations where, although it is known where and who the NR is, there are other reasons why it is felt that the NR should not be contacted. The right to respect for private and family life (Article 8 ECHR) and the right to liberty (Article 5 ECHR) are relevant here. Inappropriate usually means that there might be an interference with the patient's Article 8 ECHR rights which, in the circumstances, should take precedence over any benefit of accessing the NRs views. An obvious example would be where there is a history of conflict or abuse by the NR towards the patient; no contact between them for many years; and the patient is distressed at the prospect of the NR being contacted or discovering their whereabouts. In this case, the NR is unlikely to have any views that would assist in the Tribunal proceedings and the negative impact on the patient of contacting the NR outweighs any benefit.

Impractical refers to a situation, for example, where the NR is out of the country, unavailable, their whereabouts are unknown or it is not possible to establish who the NR is. Some patients do not have an NR and this should be clearly explained in the report.

Where the author is uncertain who the NR is, or whether to contact them, it would be wise to check with the relevant MHA Administration team, see the section papers and possibly consult the Approved Mental Health Professional (AMHP) that completed the application. The AMHP will have had to identify (or attempt to identify) the NR on the relevant section papers. It is also possible that the situation has changed since the AMHP was involved.

As we saw in Chapter 2 the NR holds specific legal powers, and may have a very important role in the patient's admission and discharge planning.

Section 117 aftercare

Section 117 MHA places a legal duty on the relevant Health Authority and Local Authority to provide or arrange for the provision of aftercare services to eligible patients. They can do so in co-operation with any relevant voluntary agencies.

Aftercare is defined in s.117(6) as services that have both of the following purposes:

a. *meeting a need arising from or related to the person's mental disorder; and*

b. *reducing the risk of a deterioration of the person's mental condition (and, accordingly, reducing the risk of the person requiring admission to a hospital again for treatment for mental disorder).*

In situations where there is a dispute about which agencies are responsible or what they will agree to provide, details of this should be set out in the report along with any steps taken to resolve this.

CTO patients cannot be discharged from s.117 aftercare for the duration of the CTO (s.117(2)).

Social circumstances report – inpatients (Category A Para 14 England and Wales)

Paragraph	Key points
England Para (d) *The patient's home and family circumstances;* *Para (e)* *The housing or accommodation available to the patient if discharged;* *Para (f)* *The patient's financial position (including benefit entitlements);* *Para (g)* *Any available opportunities for employment.* *Wales Schedule 1, Part B Para 2 (a)–(d)* *Para (c)* *Availability of community support, the relevant medical facilities.*	Both England and Wales set out their requirements slightly differently, but they are broadly the same in relation to the patient's social circumstances. These are key areas where a patient might be able to be discharged from detention if the aftercare and social support was in place. What, if any, housing is now or will be made available and what type (residential care, sheltered housing, independent living or their own tenancy, etc.)? The financial position might include whether the patient is subject to appointeeship and if there is any Lasting Power of Attorney (LPA) or Court-appointed deputy. If there has been financial exploitation or debts, what steps have been taken to manage this? In Wales, the Care and Treatment Plan should include this.
England Para (h) and Wales Para (d) *The patient's previous response to community support or section 117 aftercare.* *England Para (j) and Wales Para (e)* *So far as is known, details of the care pathway and s.117 aftercare to be made available to the patient, together with the proposed care plan.* *England Para (j)* *The likely adequacy and effectiveness of the proposed care plan.*	This is likely to form part of a wider review under whatever care pathway is appropriate, e.g. Care Programme Approach (CPA). Details of any pre-discharge plans become especially important where the patient could potentially be discharged if aftercare were in place. Where there has been a referral to a funding Panel for residential or other care, the details of when that was made, timescales and outcomes should also be available to the Tribunal.

(Continued)

(Continued)

Paragraph	Key points
	Many Local Authority and NHS areas function differently when arranging aftercare (e.g. funding and review Panels, referrals for housing or specialist support etc.) In all cases, the author of the report should be able to explain the usual process and timescales. This is an area where adjournments and requests for further information might happen. Information in the SCR should be as complete as possible.
	Although there is no specific heading, where there have been Multi-agency Risk Assessment Conferences (MARAC) or Channel and Prevent Multi-Agency meetings, this should be referenced with the relevant details. Channel and Prevent guidance can be accessed here: www.gov.uk/government/publications/channel-and-prevent-multi-agency-Panel-pmap-guidance.
England Para (r) and Wales Para (n) *Whether the patient is known to any Multi-Agency Public Protection Arrangements (MAPPA) meeting or agency and, if so, in which area, for what reason, and at what level together with the name of the Chair of any MAPPA meeting concerned with the patent, and the name of the representative of the lead agency.* *In the event of any MAPPA meeting or agency.* *And:* *England Para (s) and Wales Para (o)* *In the event that a MAPPA meeting or agency wishes to put forward evidence of its views in relation to the level and management of risk, a summary of those views (or an Executive Summary may be attached to the report); and where relevant, a copy of the Police National Computer record of previous convictions should be attached.*	The Multi-Agency Public Protection Arrangements (MAPPA) may only be relevant to some patients, but details of what level of MAPPA a patient is subject to, which area they are known to, and the reason should all be included in the reports. MAPPA can apply to both restricted and unrestricted patients. Even in situations where the patient is managed at Level 1 (by a single agency) there should still be information sharing between relevant agencies, and confirmation of this should be provided to the Tribunal. The current MAPPA guidance: 'Multi-Agency Public Protection Arrangements (MAPPA): Guidance' can be accessed here: www.gov.uk/government/publications/multi-agency-public-protection-arrangements-mappa-guidance.

Social circumstances reports – community patients (Category B Para 19 England and Wales)

Many of the headings above for inpatients are also requirements for reports on community patients (CTO patients). The English PD repeat these headings for each category of patients. The Welsh PD also refers the author to Paras (a) to (d) of Schedule 1, Part B Para 2.

In the relevant grids below, we focus on Para 19 and the paragraphs for community patients that require further explanation. Please note that the RC reports also have some similar headings and additional information worth referring back to.

Paragraph	Key points
England Para (h) and Wales Para (c) *Details of the patient's compliance with the conditions imposed under s17B and of any incidents where the patient has been recalled to hospital under s17E but where the CTO has not been revoked under s17F.*	Details of both the mandatory and discretionary conditions and the patient's response to these. Patients are sometimes recalled from CTOs even when they have been compliant with the care plan, and this should be made clear.
Wales Para (e) *Whether, in the professional opinion of the report writer, it continues to be necessary that the Responsible Clinician should be able to exercise the power of recall and, if so, why.*	There is no similar heading for the SCR in the PD for England as this heading is only within the RCs report. However, a Care Coordinator is likely to be asked their professional opinion on the necessity of recall. If you have a different opinion from the RC about the necessity of the recall power, your professional opinion is as important as the RCs. It is, of course, best to have these discussions with the RC ahead of the hearing. You can expect that the Tribunal Panel and legal representative will have noted a difference of opinion and may wish to explore this in some detail.
England Para (w) and Wales Para 14(s) *(inpatient reports)* *Whether, and if so how, any risks could be managed effectively in the community.*	Whether risks could be managed without the necessity for a CTO.

Social circumstances report – Guardianship patients (Category C Para 24 England and Wales)

Many of the headings above for inpatients are also requirements for reports on Guardianship patients. The English PD repeat these headings for each category of patients. The Welsh PD also refers the author to Paras (a) to (d) of Schedule 1, Part B, Para 2.

Following on from this, see below for subsequent paragraphs specific to Guardianship patients.

Paragraph	Key points
England Para (h) and Wales Para (d) *any requirements to which the patient is subject under section 8(1) and details of the patient's compliance.*	Details of s.8 requirements can be found in the above section titled Responsible Clinician's Reports (RC reports for Guardianship patients).

(Continued)

(Continued)

Paragraph	Key points
	The Care Coordinator and/or Guardian will have specific information on these requirements and how well they are working in practice. Which of the requirements are being used? Do they remain necessary? Have less restrictive options been ruled out?
	Has it been necessary to retake the patient to a place they are required to reside?
England Para (q) and Wales Para (l) *The views of the Guardian.*	The Guardian is likely to be the Local Authority (LA) and therefore a social worker or AMHP within the LA. In some cases, there may be a private Guardian.
	The Guardian's views are essential. It may be that the Guardian is the SCR author. However, if not, the views of the Guardian on how any of the Guardianship requirements are working and whether the same could be achieved without the powers of the Guardian are important. If the patient has not adhered to the requirements, why not?
England Para (w) and Wales Para (r) *Whether it is necessary for the welfare of the patient, or for the protection of others, that the patient should remain under Guardianship and, if so why.*	See the RC report guidance in the above section on Responsible Clinician's Reports for an explanation of 'welfare'. The Guardian's views should also be sought on this paragraph, unless they are also the author of the report.
	The author may wish to include any relevant issues related to exploitation of the patient, safeguarding and reasons why Guardianship is necessary for the patient's wellbeing/welfare.
	Could the same be achieved in a less restrictive manner without Guardianship? If not, why not?
	Where Guardianship is in place for the protection of others, an explanation in the report of what the risks to others are and in what way Guardianship is necessary to protect others.

Social circumstances report – conditionally discharged patients (Category D Para 31 (Wales) and Para 33 (England))

The PD for Wales also requires the information set out at Schedule 1 Part D Paras 1–5. This simply requires a report from any social worker, probation officer or community psychiatric nurse responsible for the patient's care and supervision in the community. It might be, for example, that the SCR is not written by the Social Supervisor but details of the person supervising the patient in the community are crucial.

Paragraph	Key points
England Para 33(f) and Wales Para 31(f) *Any conditions currently imposed (whether by the Tribunal or the Secretary of State), and the reasons why the conditions were imposed.*	Please see above in the section on Responsible Clinician's Reports, the RCs report for conditionally discharged patients requiring exactly the same information.
England Para 33(g) and Wales Para 31(g) *Details of the patient's compliance with any past or current conditions.*	Where the author of the SCR is not the Social Supervisor, they should liaise with them and the Clinical Supervisor (RC) in order to complete this heading.
England Para 33(s) and Wales Para 31(s) *The views of any partner, family member or close friend who takes a lead role in the care and support of the patient but who is not professionally involved.*	Restricted patients do not have an NR. The views of any family and friends supporting the patient in the community are therefore of particular importance. This could include their perspectives on the patient's progress and how risks might change were the patient no longer subject to the conditions and recall power. Note, however, that those close to the patient may also have been victims of the index offence.
England Para 33(w) and Wales Para 31(v) *Whether the patient if absolutely discharged would be likely to act in a manner harmful to themselves or others, whether any such risks could be managed effectively in the community and if so, how.*	Where the author of the SCR is the Social Supervisor and/or Care Coordinator they should have a unique perspective on how manageable any risks posed by the patient would be, without any conditions or power of recall. This calls for professional judgement and the ability to refer back to evidence and facts for your view. Any risk assessments by specialist services should be integrated and any progress made, e.g. work on the index offence or victim empathy. The Tribunal is being asked to discharge the patient entirely from any legal framework and so a focus on risks and how they would be managed is essential here.
England Para 33(y) and Wales Para 31(x) *Whether, and if so the extent to which it is desirable to continue, vary and/or add to any conditions currently imposed.*	Tribunals might consider removing the conditions (leaving just the recall power) as a first step before considering an absolute discharge (see Chapter 3). This goes some way to explain the requirement in both PDs to detail whether and if so the extent to which it is desirable to continue, vary and/or add to any conditions currently imposed.

Social circumstances reports – patients under 18 (*Category E Para 35 England and Wales*)

General points

The PDs for both England and Wales require specific information in relation to all categories of patients under 18 years of age (inpatients, Guardianship, CTOs and conditionally discharged).

Both MHA Codes of Practice provide helpful details in the chapters on children and young people (ch.19) s.117 aftercare (ch.33 and ch.34) and the Tribunal (ch.12). These should prove useful to anyone looking for further detail regarding patients who are under 18.

A detailed analysis of all the relevant legislation and guidance for under 18s across both countries is beyond the scope of this book. This is a complex field where various statutes, policy and guidance sometimes apply across both England and Wales and at other times there are differing provisions. Those writing an SCR for under 18s need to have knowledge of the relevant law and policy below and to be able to apply it to the relevant headings. This might require liaison with agencies such as children's services, education and adult services, the NHS and Local Authorities and, when in doubt, knowing whom to ask for the relevant information.

The MHA Codes in England and Wales advise that those who care for patients under 18 years should be familiar with the relevant law (Code 19.2 (W), 19.4 (E)). As well as the MHA this includes the Mental Capacity Act 2005 (MCA), Human Rights Act 1998 (HRA), the Children Act 1989 and 2004 and the United Nations Convention on the Rights of the Child. In Wales, the Rights of Children and Young People (Wales) Measure 2011 and the Social Services and Wellbeing (Wales) Act 2014 will be relevant and in England, for children transitioning to adult services, the Care Act 2014 will also be relevant.

Professionals working with children and young people with mental health issues should be specialists from CAMHS services according to both MHA Codes (19.2 (W), 19.4 (E)). Those writing the relevant SCR should understand the issues specific to this group of patients.

> *Para (a) People with parental responsibility and how this was acquired.*
>
> *Parental responsibility is defined in section 3(1) of the Children Act 1989 as 'all the rights, duties, powers, responsibilities and authority which by law a parent of a child has in relation to the child and his property.'*

Those who have parental responsibility have a central role in relation to decisions about the admission and treatment of their child (Code 19.6 (W), 19.7 (E)). Chapter 19 of both Codes sets out additional details of who may have PR and how it is acquired.

> *Para (b) Which public bodies either have worked together or need to liaise in relation to aftercare services that may be provided under Section 117 of the Act.*

We have already looked more generally at s.117, which applies to all ages. Not all children or young people will be eligible for s.117, but there are likely to be other legal provisions for discharge planning that the Tribunal need to be informed of.

Discussion of aftercare arrangements involving the Local Authority and other relevant agencies, should take place in advance of the Tribunal (Code 33.11 (E), 33.10(W)). Additional factors will need to be considered in relation to s.117 and children and young people. The MHA Code at Para 19.111 (E) states that:

> *This may include ensuring that the aftercare integrates with any existing provision made for looked after children and those with special education needs or disabilities, as well as safeguarding vulnerable children. Whether or not s.117 of the Act applies a child or young person who has been admitted to hospital for assessment and/or treatment of their mental disorder may be a 'child in need' for the purpose of s.17 of the Children Act 1989.*

It is likely that aftercare will involve several agencies and the Tribunal should be made aware of all plans. Agencies involved might include the relevant Local Authority team(s) from Education or from Children Services, including possibly Educational Need and Disabilities (SEND), Leaving Care, Child Protection and Adult Social Care (if transitioning to adult services). Adult services might include specialist learning disability teams. Local Authority housing departments, youth offending teams and the probation service may also be involved.

Within the NHS, apart from primary services such as the GP, children and young people who are subject to the MHA will probably be known to CAMHS (Child and Adolescent Mental Health Services). These are specialist NHS services and might include, for example, Learning Disability CAMHS teams. There may need to be liaison between CAMHS and Adult Services within the relevant NHS area when a young person is transitioning between the two.

There may be a Multi-Agency care plan or various individual plans. For example, a child or young person in England with special educational needs and disability will have an Education, Health and Care Plan (EHC) as set out in the Children and Families Act 2014.

There may be a Care, Education and Treatment Review for under 18s in England with learning disability or autism spectrum disorders (for further information see Care Education and Treatment Reviews for Children and Young People, Code and Toolkit April 2017 at www.england.nhs.uk).

In Wales, a child or young person with special educational needs and a learning difficulty and/or a disability will have an individual development plan (IDP) as set out in The Additional Learning Needs and Educational Tribunal (Wales) Act 2018 (ALNET Act). This should be a single statutory plan including any Local Health Boards or NHS Trusts consideration of treatment or services likely to be of benefit in addressing the additional learning needs and, if so, securing the provision of that treatment or service.

Those patients under 18 years in Wales who fulfil the criteria will have a Statutory Care and Treatment Plan as a result of the Mental Health (Wales) Measure 2010. For more details, see the Code of Practice to Parts 2 and 3 of the Mental Health (Wales) Measure 2010.

In certain circumstances, where patients from Wales might be placed in England, see MHA (E) Code of Practice Para 34.24–27.

For children and young people in England there will be a care plan under the CPA or relevant care pathway and in particular note MHA Code (E) Para 34.20.

In both England and Wales there may be a 'small number of children and young people who may have very complex health needs' which meet the threshold for Continuing Care (Para 2.1 of The Children and Young People's Continuing Care Guidance – January 2020 (Welsh Government) and Para 1 of the National Framework for Children and Young Peoples' Continuing Care – January 2016 (Department of Health – England)).

The provision of 'Continuing Care' is to be differentiated from NHS Continuing Healthcare, which applies to over 18s. Continuing care is in addition to the services provided by, for example, CAMHS for this small group of children or young people with additional complex needs.

The guidance in both Wales and in England supports the development of a Multi-Agency plan that synchronises assessments and care plans where possible.

> *Para (h) Whether the patient's needs have been assessed under the Children Act 1989, the Chronically Sick and Disabled Persons Act 1970 or the Social Services and Wellbeing (Wales) Act 2014 and if not, the reasons why such an assessment has not been carried out and whether it is proposed to carry out such an assessment.*

And:

> *Para (i) If there has been such an assessment, what needs or requirements have been identified and how those needs or requirement will be met.*

These two paragraphs are self-explanatory, in that they set out the relevant applicable statute, requiring the author to detail what assessments have been carried out and explain the situation where they have not. The duty to carry out any such assessment as above is with the relevant Local Authority.

Note that although the PD for England does not explicitly refer to the Care Act 2014 this is because the current PD is dated 2013. Whereas the Welsh PD is dated 2019 and therefore incorporates the relevant provisions in the Social Services and Wellbeing (Wales) Act 2014.

For young people in England transitioning to adult services, young carers and any carer of the child, the relevant sections of the Care Act (s.58–s.64) will apply. MHA Code (E) Para 19.119 states that:

> *Young people's transition from CAMHS requires careful planning, which should start at least six months before the young person is due to leave CAMHS …*
>
> *Para (j) If the patient is subject to or has been the subject of a Care Order or an interim Care Order*
>
> *I. The date and duration of any such order*
> *II. Identity of the relevant Local Authority*

    III.   *Identity of any person(s) with whom the Local Authority shares parental responsibility*

    IV.   *Whether there are any proceedings that have yet to conclude and, if so, the Court in which proceedings are taking pace and the date of the next hearing.*

See Part IV of the Children Act 1989 and s.31–s.40. It should be straightforward to confirm with the relevant Local Authority whether a child is or has been subject to any care orders.

    V.   *Whether the patient comes under the Children (Leaving Care) Act 2000 or the Social Services and Wellbeing (Wales) Act 2014.*

Under these statutes, the relevant Local Authority responsible for the young person aged 16–17 years old is under a duty to assess and meet the needs of those young people leaving care.

    VI.   *Whether there has been any liaison between, on the one hand, social workers responsible for mental health services to children and adolescents and, on the other hand, those responsible for such services to adults.*

This should be self-explanatory. See Para (h) and (i) above.

    VII.   *The name of the social worker with the relevant Local Authority who is discharging the function of the Nearest Relative under section 27 of the Act:*

Which states:

> *Where a child or young person is in the care of a Local Authority by virtue of a care order within the meaning of the Children Act 1989 ... that authority shall be deemed to be the Nearest Relative of the patient in preference to any person except the patient's husband or wife or civil partner (if any).*

> *Para (l) If the patient is a Ward of Court, when the patient was made a Ward of Court and what steps have been taken to notify the Court that made the order of any significant steps taken, or to be taken, in respect of the patient.*

Where a child is made a Ward of Court under the Court's inherent jurisdiction this means the Court has custody of the child and must consent to any important decisions concerning the child, including decisions under the MHA (see s.33 MHA).

> *Para (m) Whether any other orders under the Children Act 1989 are in existence in respect of the patient, and, if so, the details of those orders, together with the date on which such orders were made, and whether they are final or interim orders.*

The MHA Code (19.8 (E), 19.6 (W)) sets out the likely range of orders under the Children Act 1989, recommending checking medical and social services files for any child arrangements orders (s.8), special Guardianship orders (s.14), appointment as a Guardian for the child or young person (s.5), parental responsibility agreements or orders under s.4 Children Act 1989 and any Wardships.

Para (n) Looked after children (this paragraph details relevant statutory obligations in Wales and England).

Section 20 of the Children Act 1989 places a duty on the Local Authority to provide accommodation for any child in need in their area who requires accommodation as a result of either no one holding parental responsibility for them, being lost or having been abandoned or where the person providing care is being prevented for whatever reason from proving suitable accommodation or care. This could include the provision of specialist accommodation where parents agree to the placement of their child in that accommodation to meet a specific need, e.g. residential school for a child with a learning disability and complex needs.

See also s.67 of the Social Services and Wellbeing (Wales) Act 2014 for the same duty in Wales.

Schedule 2 of the Children Act 1989 applies to England only.

Paragraph 17(1) has now been repealed by the Children and Young Persons Act 2008, and s.16 requires independent visitors for children looked after by a Local Authority. A similar provision in Wales is within s.98 of the Social Services and Wellbeing (Wales) Act 2014.

Paragraph 10(b) of Schedule 2 of the Children Act 1989 is the duty to take such steps as are reasonably practicable where any child is living apart from their family to promote contact between him and his family. The same provision in Wales is within s.39(2) of the Social Services and Wellbeing (Wales) Act 2014.

Para (p) If a patient has been the subject of a secure accommodation order under s.25 of the Children Act 1989, the date on which the order was made, the reasons it was made and the date it expired.

It is not possible for a child to be detained under the MHA at the same time as being the subject of a secure accommodation order. However, it is important to note that a secure accommodation order is for the purposes of restricting the liberty of a child or young person where there is a history of absconding and they are likely to suffer significant harm or that if kept in any other such accommodation they are likely to injure themselves or other persons. Therefore, any previous orders made under s.25 Children Act 1989 are informative for the Tribunal in decisions about aftercare and risk.

Para (q) If a patient is a child provided with accommodation under sections 85 and 86 of the Children Act what steps have been taken by the accommodating authority or the person carrying on the establishment in question to discharge their notification responsibilities and what steps have been taken by the Local Authority to discharge their obligations under sections 85, 86 and 86A of the Children Act 1989.

Sections 85 and 86 of the Children Act 1989 and s.120 of the Social Services and Wellbeing (Wales) Act 2014 makes provision for children who are accommodated by health or education authorities, independent care homes or hospitals for a consecutive period of at least three months or with the intention to accommodate them for this time. The accommodating authority will notify the relevant Local Authority.

Once notified, the relevant Local Authority must make arrangements for the child to be visited by a Local Authority representative under s.86A of the Children Act.

Also see s.116 MHA 1983 for further duties on Local Authorities to arrange visits and any other parental functions for children subject to care orders who are admitted to hospital.

Chapter 8
Pre-hearing matters

Introduction

This chapter will cover the procedural and other matters that arise in the interim period between an application or reference being made and the Tribunal hearing taking place. Some of these steps happen behind the scenes as far as clinicians are concerned, but the information may still be of use as reference material and may also help to explain why professionals might find themselves being chased by Mental Health Act Administrators for availability, reports, views on interim applications, etc. On legal documents you might come across the phrase 'interlocutory matter' or 'interlocutory decision', which simply means it is an issue that has arisen in the course of Tribunal proceedings before the final hearing.

The chapter will cover how hearings are listed and the relevant timescales that are applied; the timescales for the submission of reports; case management requests and decisions such as postponement or time extensions; capacity issues; independent experts; and pre-hearing examinations and withdrawals. Disclosure issues may arise before the hearing; see Chapter 7 for guidance on seeking to withhold information from the patient.

Most of these matters are governed by the Tribunal Rules and Practice Directions (PDs).

Listing of cases

After receiving an application or reference, in most cases the Tribunal Office will notify 'the parties', i.e. The Responsible Authority and the patient (in practice the relevant Mental Health Act Administration team and the patient or, if the patient is represented, the patient's legal representative) of the proceedings.

In England, a Case Notification Letter (CNL1) is issued to the parties. The exception is in s.2 cases: because s.2 hearings have to take place within a short timescale the formalities of the CNL1 are dispensed with and the hearing will simply be listed and the parties notified (further details below).

For non-s.2 cases, a 'listing window' will be identified in the CNL1, which simply means the period of time within which the hearing will take place. A three-week window will be defined for restricted cases and a four-week window for all other cases.

The CNL1 will also contain directions on the following matters:

- That the parties submit their availability for attending a hearing within the listing window. The parties are required to identify three full days or six half days and are usually given two weeks to provide this availability to the Tribunal Office using a hearing questionnaire (HQ1). Failure to provide this form within the time limits will mean that the hearing will be listed without regard to the defaulting party's availability – this is why clinicians might receive increasingly strident emails from their Mental Health Act Administrators chasing their availability.

- A deadline for the filing of the various reports required by the Tribunal Rules and Practice Directions.

- Notice of the procedural steps to be taken if a party (invariably the hospital) wishes to prohibit disclosure of a document or information relating to a patient or other party (see Chapter 7).

- A notice to the patient or their representative that they must use their best endeavours to ensure that a request to withdraw an application is made at least two days before the hearing. This is to assist with the administration of the Tribunal service as a whole – the more notice that is given of a withdrawal, then the less risk there is of wasted preparation time by Tribunal Panel Members (and professionals). A prompt withdrawal may also mean that Tribunal Members can be diverted to sit on alternative cases.

There is no equivalent form in Wales and matters such as listing of the hearing are dealt with by correspondence.

Timescales for hearings and reports

There are only two categories of cases that have specified timescales in the Tribunal Rules for both England and Wales: s.2 cases must start within seven days of receipt of the application or reference and, when a conditionally discharged patient is recalled to hospital, the hearing must start at least five weeks but no more than eight weeks from receipt of the reference. The Rules are silent on the timescales for all other cases such as s.3 or Community Treatment Order (CTO) cases. The Tribunal information on gov.uk says:

The date of the hearing depends on your situation. You'll usually get a hearing within:

- *7 days of applying if you've been admitted for assessment*
- *2 months if you've been admitted for treatment*
- *4 months if you've received an order from the Crown Court or been transferred from prison (known as a 'restricted patient')*

(www.gov.uk/mental-health-Tribunal/after-you-send-your-appeal)

The MHRTW guidance is very similar and says that s.2 hearings will be within seven days; restricted cases within 14 weeks and all other cases within eight weeks.

FAQ: Why do we get such short notice of s.2 hearings?

Answer: For s.2 cases, the Rules require listing within seven days and that parties are given at least three days' notice of the hearing – meaning that there may only be one or two possible dates for the hearing to take place. There has been a consultation in England as to whether the listing window should be extended to ten days.

In practice, patients can expect a s.3 matter to be listed approximately four to eight weeks from the date of the application or reference subject to possible delays if any of the interim issues discussed below arise.

The longer timescale for restricted cases is primarily because the Secretary of State (in practice the Mental Health Casework Section of the Ministry of Justice) is a 'party' in these cases and must be given at least 21 days from receipt of the reports to consider the reports and to file a statement summarising the index offence and the history of detention since the restriction order was made, along with a record of the patient's previous convictions (known colloquially as 'pre-cons'). The Secretary of State is also entitled to express a view on any recommendations in the reports but tends to take a neutral stance in most cases.

Following an application or reference, the Tribunal will require the following documents to be filed:

- A statement of information about the patient (often referred to as a 'Part A Statement'). This is factual information about the patient; involved professionals; the responsible authorities for s.117 purposes; the Nearest Relative; any history of admissions, Tribunal hearings and transfers between hospitals.

- The Responsible Clinician's (RC) report.

- The nursing report (for inpatients).

- The social circumstances reports (SCRs).

The requirements of these reports are examined in more detail in Chapter 7.

The deadlines for the filing of reports vary depending on the type of case. In England:

- For s.2 cases the reports must be provided as soon as practicable but no later than an hour before the hearing. The section papers must be provided to the Tribunal immediately on request or when the hospital receives the application. Receiving reports an hour before the hearing is less than ideal for the Panel, the patient and the legal representative but, the rule gives the maximum latitude to professionals who may have to prepare reports within a matter of days on a patient not previously known to mental health services.

- For all other cases, the general rule is that the reports must be filed with the Tribunal within three weeks of the application or reference being received or submitted by the hospital.

In Wales, the Rules are similar except that in s.2 cases, the rule is less stringent and the Responsible Authority is only required to provide any reports that can reasonably be provided in the time available.

As mentioned above, these deadlines for reports are an example of when professionals might find themselves being chased by Mental Health Act Administration teams. The Tribunal has a range of powers (Rules 7 and 10 (E), Rule 19 (W)) to enforce the Rules and, in the event of reports being late, professionals will be served with an 'Order to Answer Questions', swiftly followed by a summons to attend the hearing to explain the failure to comply with the Rules. Ultimately, the Tribunal can refer the matter to the Upper Tribunal to exercise its High Court powers to force compliance or issue a wasted costs order against the defaulting party. It would be very rare for costs orders to be issued against public authorities such as the NHS or a Local Authority but is a possibility if, for example, there is a series of adjourned or postponed hearings caused by a failure to comply with the Rules.

Questions of capacity?

The Rules only refer to 'capacity' but, for under 16s, the issue would be 'competence'. For details on assessment of competence of under 16s, see Chapter 19 of the MHA Codes. Otherwise, the issues discussed below apply to all patients regardless of age.

Issues concerning the patient's capacity can arise at any stage from the point of an application being made through to concerns cropping up during the hearing. It has become a complex area and has generated quite a large amount of case-law because, although the principles and provisions of the Mental Capacity Act 2005 (MCA) apply, the degree and depth of understanding required of the patient to make a decision varies depending on the complexity of the decision and tends to arise in two particular circumstances, as follows.

Capacity to make an application in the first place?

An invalid application can be struck out and a patient cannot make a valid application or authorise another person to make the application if they lack the capacity to do so. As one might expect, given access to the Tribunal is the key mechanism for a patient to challenge their detention, the bar for the requisite capacity has been set very low (although many would say still not low enough). To make a valid application, the patient must a) understand they are being detained against their wishes and b) that the Tribunal is a body that can decide whether they should be released (*SM v Livewell Southwest CIC* [2020]). If a patient does not understand both of these matters they cannot make a valid application. This might raise concerns that a particularly vulnerable group of patients are denied access to an independent review of their detention but, as seen in Chapter 2, the system of automatic references to the Tribunal provided for in the Mental Health Act (MHA) means that for patients without the capacity to make their own application there will be automatic periodic reviews by the Tribunal. In addition, if any professional or family member feels that a Tribunal hearing would assist an incapacitated patient, keep in mind that anyone, at any time, can ask the Secretary of State to submit a discretionary reference to the Tribunal.

Capacity to appoint a legal representative?

It is a big ask for a patient to represent themselves in legal proceedings where their liberty may be at stake and the decision as to whether to appoint a legal representative or not is an important one. It is also important to be aware that solicitors are not permitted to seek to act for a person that lacks the capacity to instruct them – for obvious ethical reasons.

If a patient with the necessary capacity decides to represent themselves, they are entitled to do so and indeed some Judges would say that the patient might be better off representing themselves than having a poor quality legal representative. But, in general, hearings probably run more smoothly with a representative present as they should be able to assist in narrowing the issues in dispute, focusing on the legal criteria and acting as something of a buffer between the patient and the professionals. If a patient represents themself, they are entitled to directly cross-examine the professionals, which might cause concerns about harm to therapeutic relationships. One might also wonder about the fairness of such a hearing bearing in mind that 'equality of arms' (that the parties are on as equal a footing as possible) is a facet of a fair trial under Article 6 ECHR. Access to appropriate legal advice and the assistance of a legal representative to present the patient's evidence and to challenge professional evidence should go some way to levelling the playing field for Article 6 purposes.

If a patient lacks the capacity to appoint a representative, the Rules provide a safeguard in that the Tribunal has the power to appoint a representative if it believes it to be in the patient's best interests. The Tribunal can also appoint a representative for a patient with capacity if they have stated they wish to be represented or that they do not wish to conduct their own case but, for whatever reason, haven't arranged representation themselves. You might encounter the phrase 'Rule 11 case', which simply means that the Tribunal have exercised their power under Rule 11 to appoint a representative. In Wales, the power to appoint is in Rule 13.

> *In relation to the capacity to appoint a representative, case-law has established the following:*
>
> - *The MCA principles and approach apply and therefore the starting point is a presumption of capacity.*
> - *The specific decision for the patient is whether or not to appoint a representative.*
> - *The level of understanding required for this decision is greater than that for deciding whether to apply to the Tribunal as discussed above.*
> - *To have capacity to decide to appoint a representative the patient would need to be able to understand, retain, use and weigh matters such as the Tribunal's powers and the opportunity to challenge a detention at a hearing; that representation is free and the representative will be able to discuss the case with the patient before the hearing; the representative might be better placed to deal with matters of fact and law, questioning of witnesses and arguing the case.*
>
> *(YA v CNWL NHS TRUST and Others [2015])*

The Rule 11 process is generally thought to work well in practice *'to further the underlying purposes of (a) Article 5 and its procedural requirements, (b) the MHA and (c) common law principles of fairness'* (ibid.). If a representative is appointed to act for a patient lacking capacity, they have a heightened duty to act in the best (legal) interests of their client and to assist the Tribunal to test the criteria for detention even if the patient cannot express any wishes or feelings about their circumstances.

In practice, if the Tribunal receives an application or reference and there is no indication that the patient is represented they will direct that a capacity statement (in relation to the patient's capacity to appoint a representative) be completed by the RC in order to ascertain whether an appointment of a representative is required. This practice has attracted criticism as being a potential conflict of interest for the RC who is usually arguing for the patient's continued detention and may therefore have an interest in not being cross-examined by a legal representative and could be tempted to lean towards assessing the patient as having the capacity to decide to represent themselves (see Jones, 2020, p863).

ACTIVITY 8.1

Can you list the situations where an assessment of the patient's capacity might be required in the course of Tribunal proceedings?

Case management requests

Various issues might arise between an application or reference being made and the hearing taking place and the Tribunal may be asked to make a particular decision or direction. In England these are dealt with on a standard form called a case management request. Generally, these will be completed by MHA Administrators or the patient's legal representative. The Tribunal can be asked to take any decision or action within their powers and will apply the overriding objective of the Tribunal Rules, which is to deal with cases fairly and justly.

The most common requests are included on the form and are:

- Postponement of the hearing might be required because, for example, the patient has transferred to a new hospital; an unforeseen clash of commitments has arisen; an important assessment or review is pending.

- A direction prohibiting disclosure of a document or information to another party. Most commonly, this is where there is a wish to withhold sensitive information in the professionals' reports from the patient (see Chapter 7).

- A pre-hearing examination (PHE) by the Medical Member of the Tribunal (see below). These requests will always be agreed up to 14 days before the hearing. Any late requests will require a case management request and further explanation. In Wales, PHEs are automatic in every case.

- Withdrawal of an application (see below).

Other common requests are for disclosure of particular documents or clinical notes; a time extension for the filing of reports; a direction that a specific person attend the hearing to give evidence – for example, the legal representative might consider it essential that the author of a report rather than a colleague attend the hearing to answer questions; a request for an interpreter to be provided if this was not requested on the application or reference.

If professionals anticipate any difficulties with the timing of the hearing or any practical arrangements for the hearing it would be sensible to discuss this with your MHA Administration team as it may be that the Tribunal can assist by issuing appropriate directions.

Withdrawal and reinstatement (Rule 17 (E) and Rule 22 (W))

The Tribunal's consent is required to withdraw an application and they will need to be satisfied that a review of the detention is not required (*AMA v Greater Manchester West Mental Health NHS Foundation Trust* [2015]). It is not unusual for patients to be changeable about whether they wish to pursue a potentially stressful contested hearing. Patients might decide to withdraw because of some progress with their care and treatment, such as being granted unescorted leave or a community placement being identified. Patients may also re-evaluate the merits of their application having read the Tribunal reports or having received legal advice. A withdrawn application means that the patient can apply again at a later date.

Whilst it can be frustrating for professionals who spend a large amount of time preparing a Tribunal report only for the patient to withdraw their application, sometimes very close to the hearing date or even at the hearing itself, it is obviously important that the patient has the opportunity to change their mind about pursuing an application given that only one application can be made in each period of detention. The later that a request to withdraw is made, the greater the Tribunal will scrutinise the reasons for it.

Note that statutory references to the Tribunal cannot be withdrawn. It might seem surprising that a hearing will proceed when a patient has not asked for it and may even be actively opposed to it but remember that the system of automatic references is there as a safeguard to ensure at least periodic review of the use of MHA powers.

If the Tribunal consent to a withdrawal, then the case is closed and the hearing cancelled. In England only, the patient may apply for the case to be reinstated. This is at the discretion of the Tribunal. The only circumstances when this would have an advantage over simply making a new application is if the patient has entered into a new period of eligibility (because the section has been renewed or a CTO extended) and already has a new right to apply again but wishes to preserve this and make use of their original application first.

Pre-hearing examinations

This is the procedure by which the Medical Member of the Tribunal will examine the patient to form an opinion on their mental condition (Rule 34 (E), Rule 20 (W)). See Chapter 4 for details of the pre-hearing examination (PHE) process.

In Wales, PHEs take place if practicable (i.e. if the patient cooperates with the process) in every case. In England, PHEs will always take place in s.2 cases, but in all other cases a request for a PHE needs to be made in advance of the hearing. If the request is made at least 14 days before the hearing, then this will be granted without question. Requests made less than 14 days before the hearing will require further explanation about the need for a PHE. In most cases these requests will be dealt with by the legal representative following discussion with the patient about the merits of requesting a PHE or not.

> ### EXPERT QUOTE
>
> *I think that PHEs are a way of demonstrating to the patient the complete independence of the Panel. I think that they are essential in section 2 cases as the patients' mental state can change so quickly and diagnoses may not be clearly established. I think in CAMHS cases and Tribunals where the patient is not likely to be able to sit calmly through the other evidence they are essential as a way of building up rapport so that the patient knows that they can go into the Tribunal not being faced by three strangers.*

Independent experts

To challenge a particular diagnosis, risk formulation, aftercare plan or other key piece of professional evidence, the patient (usually via their legal representative) may instruct an independent expert to provide a report and possibly attend the hearing to give evidence. Most often, this would be an independent psychiatric report, but other independent professionals such as psychologists, occupational therapists or social workers might also be instructed to prepare a report. The expert has a right to visit and examine the patient and to inspect any relevant records (s.76 MHA). The expert may seek to discuss the case with the relevant professional to identify any particular differences of opinion or areas of agreement ahead of the hearing.

Legal Aid is available for these expenses in the context of Tribunal proceedings. Fees for independent experts are at a rate fixed by regulations and the Legal Aid Agency require detailed justification as to why an expert is required in a particular case. Anecdotally, it appears that the use of such experts in Tribunal cases is reducing.

> **Top tips**
>
> - *Bear in mind that there are 'listing windows' that require you to provide availability to the Tribunal. Once you have done this, it would be sensible to diarise the dates you have offered.*
>
> - *Make sure you comply with the deadlines for submitting your report.*
>
> - *Where you wish to withhold information in your report from the patient look at Chapter 7.*
>
> - *Independent experts will have read your report and the patients' records in preparation for the hearing. They may wish to speak with you.*

Chapter summary

- Section 2 hearings must take place within seven days of the application or reference.

- In s.2 cases, professionals' reports must be available no less than one hour before the hearing (in England). In all other cases the reports must be filed within three weeks of the application or reference. An extension can be requested but justification would be required.

- Questions about the patient's capacity may arise at any stage in the Tribunal proceedings. There is provision for legal representatives to be appointed by the Tribunal when the patient has not or cannot appoint a representative themselves.

- The Tribunal has a wide range of case management powers and the parties can make written case management requests at any stage before the final hearing.

- The Medical Member of the Tribunal may conduct a pre-hearing examination of the patient ahead of a hearing.

- The patient may instruct their own independent experts in order to challenge professional evidence.

Chapter 9
What happens at the hearing?

Introduction

This chapter will look at what might happen on the day of the hearing, including any pre-liminary matters that require attention on the day before the hearing starts. It will then explain the usual order of evidence, likely questions that will be asked and why. There is a pictorial guide to the usual seating arrangements for face-to-face hearings.

Where does the Tribunal take place?

The usual venue will be the hospital where the patient is detained. In the case of patients in the community (subject to a Community Treatment Order (CTO), Guardianship or a con-ditional discharge) the venue could be a community base or residential establishment where the patient resides.

Technically, a hearing could take place at a Court venue with witnesses and parties asked to attend there. However, to meet the needs of patients, Tribunals will take place where the patient is. The Tribunal:

> tries hard to give patients and their relatives easy access to the Tribunal which is itself designed to meet their needs' and 'they are designed to be user friendly and to allow the patient and relative to communicate directly with the Tribunal.

> (R(H) v SSH [2006])

Hence the Tribunal will come to the patient rather than the patient having to attend a central Tribunal venue. There are, however, minimum standards for safety and security that the Tribunal expects when attending a venue on-site and Hospital Managers and Mental Health Act (MHA) Administration teams should be aware of these (for England see HMCTS Minimum Requirements for Tribunal Hearings to be Held in Hospitals. April 2018).

Private or public hearings?

The Tribunal Rules stipulate that all hearings must be held in private unless a patient requests a hearing in public. The Rules slightly vary between England and Wales and the Tribunal will agree the request if satisfied that this would be in the interest of the patient (Wales) or justice (England) (Rule 38 (E), Rule 25 (W)). Even on the rare occasion that a hearing is public, part of it could still be held in private – these decisions rest with the Tribunal. Attendees will not be permitted to make notes unless expressly allowed by the Tribunal. Furthermore, it is a criminal offence to record a hearing and those in attendance will probably be reminded before the start that the proceedings are confidential.

Preparatory matters and practicalities

The Panel will be in attendance ahead of the start time for the hearing. They are advised to be available for face-to-face hearings at least an hour before the start time to deal with any preliminary matters arising on the day and to hear feedback from any pre-hearing examination (PHE) by the Medical Member.

The following professionals may also be in attendance ahead of the hearing:

- Tribunal Clerk (if a clerk has been made available – where there is no clerk, often the hospital's MHA Administration team take on the clerking role for the Tribunal. However, it is also possible that there is no clerk or administrator and the Panel deals with practicalities themselves);

- Any interpreter will be nearby (possibly on the ward with the patient);

- The patient's representative (again possibly on the ward with the patient).

The Panel should have been given a list of those attending the hearing and be made aware of any issues arising, e.g. family or friends attending and if so, in what role, any victims' representations and anyone else who wishes or has requested to attend (e.g. requests by observers).

The Panel should have received the required reports. They will also have any additional information submitted, such as any previous Tribunal decisions, statements from the Ministry of Justice for restricted patients and any other statements or relevant documents. Except in s.2 cases, reports are sent to Tribunal Panel Members in advance of the hearing. In s.2 cases the Tribunal must be sent the medical recommendations and application authorising the detention. Further information and reports should be sent as soon as possible and might include any report written by the Approved Mental Health Professional (AMHP) who completed the application for admission. Where these reports are made available on the day of the hearing, Panel Members are required to read and digest these and raise any matters and questions they might have before the hearing starts.

Prior to the hearing start time there might be a range of preliminary matters arising that require resolution before the hearing can begin.

Preliminary matters

It may be puzzling that some professionals go into the hearing before it begins and ahead of others. We have heard professionals express some confusion at the 'coming and going' by various people in and out of the Tribunal room before the hearing starts.

It can be frustrating to arrive on time, only to be kept waiting past the start time for the hearing. This may happen if the Tribunal was not informed about something relevant in advance or something unforeseeable occurs on the day. However, various issues or preliminary matters might arise that the Tribunal will need to attend to before the hearing starts. Below is a list of common matters that might arise.

PHE: The Panel is required to hear the details of any PHE that has taken place.

Venue issues and risk: There may be issues raised ahead of the hearing over the suitability of the venue. In some circumstances, where the patient is unable to leave the ward due to risks, the hearing may need to take place on the ward. The suitability of the room and risk issues will then need to be considered and managed.

Missing patients: The patient may have gone absent without leave (AWOL) or have decided not to attend the hearing or have become too unwell to be able to state their wishes. All such issues will require resolution by the Tribunal in liaison with any representative for the patient and the hospital staff.

Capacity issues on the day: It might be that the representative requires appointing by the Tribunal if the patient is now considered to lack the capacity to do so. The representative might ask to see the Panel if they have been unable to see the patient or take instructions. This can be done on the day but will require assessment of the patient's capacity. It is likely that the Medical Member will be asked to see the patient (possibly as part of the PHE) to assess their capacity to appoint a representative and there may be consultation with the Responsible Clinician (RC) before the Panel make a decision.

The representative or the MHA Administrator might wish to see the Panel ahead of the actual hearing to explain various things. For example, they may wish to tell the Panel that the patient's family wants to attend or that the patient does not wish to attend or that someone else has requested to observe the hearing.

The Tribunal may wish to see the patient's representative if they have any matters that need to be dealt with before the full hearing starts. The Panel may wish to discuss the order of evidence, for example, if the Medical Member had concerns from the PHE about the patient's ability to manage the hearing, it may be suggested to the representative that the patient gives their evidence at the beginning of the hearing. The Panel may wish to seek the views of the representative about any procedural difficulties that have arisen, such as missing reports or a witness unable to attend or some other point of law that has arisen; it would be usual for the RC to also be involved in these preliminary discussions.

Requests to withhold information: Ideally, issues around disclosure of information to the patient should be resolved ahead of the hearing in keeping with the duty under the Rules to assist the Tribunal to deal with the case fairly and justly – which includes avoiding delay (See Rule 2 (E), Rule 3 (W) and *Dorset Healthcare NHS Foundation Trust v MH* [2009]). However, the issue might arise on the day of the hearing rather than in advance, perhaps as a result of a late written report or lack of liaison between professionals. This might necessitate some detailed discussion with the relevant professionals and the patient's representative. A decision will need to be made by the Panel before the hearing can proceed. For further information on disclosure and withholding of information from the patient (see Chapter 7).

ACTIVITY 9.1

Consider the following scenario:

The Panel has arrived for a hearing at the hospital. The MHA Administrator informs them that the RC wishes to withhold specific information from the patient.

The Panel and the patient's representative already have a full set of reports.

The social circumstances report has details of the very issue that the RC had requested be withheld.

As a result, the Tribunal asks to see the RC and explain the situation as the reports have already been shared with the patient by the representative.

The RC had written the report late and had not read the other reports. They agreed in hindsight that it was now too late to withhold the information and that his request could not be granted.

Question:

* *How could the above scenario have been averted? Note down your thoughts.*

Adjournments

At any point, the Tribunal could adjourn, which usually means that the Panel has convened, but the hearing is not to go ahead for various reasons, for example, a key witness being absent or a report not having been filed with the Tribunal in time.

The patient's representative should be included in these discussions and reasons given if the Tribunal decides to adjourn. In many cases, this might be as a result of a request from the patient's representative. For example, there is insufficient information or key information or witnesses are absent. If the patient has not yet instructed a representative but indicates a last-minute wish to be represented the hearing might be adjourned in order for this to take place.

The hearing

The formal Rules of evidence in Court proceedings do not apply to the Tribunal and so there are no set rules for how the hearing will run or evidence will be heard. The informality and flexibility is to ensure the patient is enabled to participate as fully as possible and is not overly intimidated or stressed by the proceedings. Having said that, others present are expected to adhere to a level of formality and respect in their conduct.

The remainder of the chapter describes the usual process in most hearings with the caveat that sometimes the Tribunal might vary this and hear evidence in a different order. The Rules give a large amount of flexibility to the Tribunal in managing the procedure so that a hearing can be conducted in the best manner for each case.

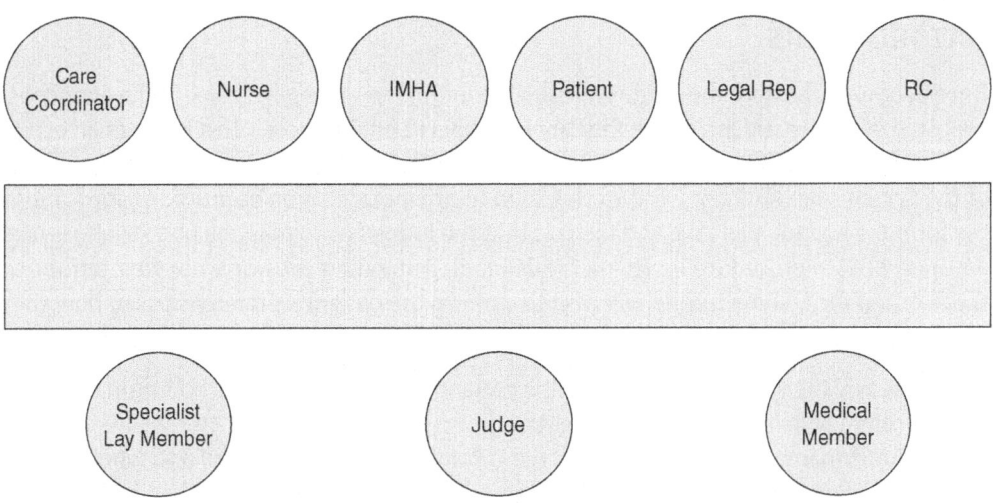

Figure 9.1   A typical seating arrangement in a Tribunal hearing

Seating plans

The Tribunal Clerk, MHA Administrator or a Panel Member will invite all witnesses into the hearing.

The Panel will have the Judge in the centre, with the Medical Member to their right and Specialist Lay Member (SpLM) to their left.

Those attending as witnesses will usually sit across from the Panel Members most likely to question them first. So, for example, the RC will sit opposite the Medical Member and the inpatient nurse will sit next to the RC. The author of the social circumstances report will sit opposite the SpLM and the patient, and their representative will sit in the middle.

If any expert witnesses are in attendance, they will usually sit next to the relevant witness (e.g. a medical expert witness will sit next to the RC and a social work expert witness next to the author of the SCR).

If an Independent Mental Health Advocate (IMHA) is in attendance they will usually sit next to the patient on the opposite side from the patient's representative.

An interpreter will, of course, have to sit next to the patient.

Any family members there to support or other observers will usually be asked to sit behind or to the side of the witnesses. There are a number of potential attendees; please refer back to Chapter 5 for more detail.

This is the most likely arrangement you will encounter, but the Panel can be flexible so, for example, the patient might be seated closest to the exit either at their own request or for risk management purposes – making it easier for the patient to leave or be escorted from the room in the event of becoming distressed or agitated.

Introductions

Once everyone is seated, the Judge will usually confirm the names and roles of the attendees, welcome everyone and introduce the Panel Members and their roles. This includes an explanation of the role of the Tribunal with emphasis on the fact that the Tribunal is independent of the Responsible Authority. This explanation might include some basic information about the form the hearing will take and the fact that the Judge has to manage note-taking whilst ensuring proper procedure – often a preamble to reminding everyone not to interrupt or speak out of turn. Some Judges will wish to confirm the patient's preference as to how they wish to be addressed.

The Judge will then usually ensure that the patient's representative has had sight of all the same written evidence as the Panel (i.e. the professional reports, any statements or other relevant documents that were filed with the Tribunal before the hearing) and whether they have any preference as to the order of evidence (if this has not been discussed already). The Tribunal will usually follow the patient's preference as to when they give their evidence, and there would usually have been discussion between the patient and their representative about this. It is a tricky judgement as, whilst there is obviously some advantage to the patient of hearing all of the professional evidence before speaking to the Panel, some patients may struggle to have to sit through lengthy professional opinion that they may vehemently disagree with without having their say or may be understandably anxious about the hearing and may benefit from being able to speak at an early stage of the proceedings. See Chapter 10 for further detail on the patient's welfare.

Feedback from the PHE

Following introductions, in cases where there has been a PHE, the content of this will be fed back to everyone either by the Judge or directly from the Medical Member.

The Judge may then seek to confirm and, if possible, narrow the issues in discussion with the representative or by the representative making a brief opening statement dealing with the applications being pursued (discharge, recommendations for leave or transfer, etc.) and which of the legal criteria are in dispute. This simply means clarifying for the Panel which parts of the legal criteria the patient disagrees with and if there are any of the criteria that the patient would accept as correct.

This can be a useful process for the patient, the Panel and for the professional witnesses; for example, if the patient is accepting of their diagnosis but wishes to remain in hospital informally then it may mean that questions on the issue of mental disorder do not need to be laboured and everyone can focus on the key issue of the necessity for detention.

Addressing the Panel

Because the Tribunal is a Court on the one hand but also seeking to minimise formality on the other, those attending a hearing can be left feeling anxious about how to properly address the Panel Members. You will not find anything in the law, the Rules or the Practice Directions about this and indeed Judges vary in how formally they wish to be addressed.

The correct term of address for a Tribunal Judge would be Sir or Madam (see: www.judiciary. uk/you-and-the-judiciary/what-do-i-call-judge/), and most Judges, in our experience, would be content to simply be addressed as Judge. The Medical Member would obviously be 'Doctor' and for the SpLM, you will need to listen out during introductions for their title.

> ### EXPERT QUOTE
>
> *Appropriate attire – you are in Court. Appropriate mode of address – Sir/Madam to the Panel Members.*

The patient's evidence

The Panel will take the patient's evidence by inviting the representative to put questions to them or to allow the patient to put forward their case directly if they are not represented. The representative's role is to assist the patient to put forward their case for whatever it is they are asking the Tribunal to do (discharge, make a recommendation, etc.); to draw out the positive aspects of the patient's case and to deal with any disputed matters in the reports. The representative knows the information that is likely to be of importance to the Tribunal's decision making on the statutory criteria and will try to focus on this. It can be understandably difficult for some patients to maintain this focus as they may feel very aggrieved at their detention and wish to take the opportunity to vent their general dissatisfaction with the hospital or professionals.

Panel Members will usually try to avoid questions that have already been answered by the patient or are on matters that are clear in the reports and not disputed. The patient is not on trial (and remember that in most cases the 'burden' is on the Responsible Authority to make their case, not the patient), but the Panel will need to 'test the evidence' themselves in order to come to independent conclusions (i.e. to evaluate the facts and opinion being put forward by the professionals and the patient). If the legal representative has been thorough when dealing with the patient's evidence, it may be that the Panel have few further questions for the patient, and they will usually be alert to the wellbeing of the patient and avoid unnecessary or duplicate questions.

Questioning of professionals

Prior to the professionals being questioned, they will usually be asked in turn to confirm that they have read the report if they did not write it and whether or not they agree with the content.

Professionals should be prepared to answer questions such as how long they have known the patient, when they last saw them, what their role is (e.g. RC, primary nurse or Care Coordinator etc.) and whether they wish to add to or update anything in the report.

It is important for professionals to remember that, in answering questions from the Panel, they are giving evidence to the Tribunal, and answers should be directed to the Panel Member who asked the question. In the interests of trying to maintain their relationship with the patient, professionals sometimes understandably fall into the trap of addressing their evidence to the patient or trying to engage in a dialogue with the patient, which may lead to a rebuke from the Judge.

> ## EXPERT QUOTE
>
> *When giving oral evidence be clear, concise and accurate. If you do not understand the question put to you by either the Tribunal Panel or the legal representative, do ask for the question to be clarified. If you do not know the answer, or are unsure, say so – this will put you in a stronger position than trying to answer a question when you either do not understand it, or do not know the answer.*
>
> *When giving evidence answer the question that you are being asked, not the question that you would like to have been asked.*

The order of the professional evidence is not defined and is at the discretion of the Panel. We have referred to the RC throughout the chapter but, in many cases, the medical evidence might be given by a covering colleague or trainee doctor on behalf of the RC. In most cases the Panel will wish to hear from the RC first – the RC has the power to discharge the patient (s.23 MHA) and therefore they will be asked explicitly about the statutory criteria and which grounds are relied on for continued detention or community compulsion.

Some Judges will go through the criteria with the RC at an early stage of the hearing as part of the process of narrowing the issues for the Panel to concentrate on. Although the focus will be on the RC's evidence in relation to the statutory criteria, the other professionals in attendance might be asked to express a view on these matters. For example, a social circumstances report author with experience of working with the patient in the community might be very well placed to give evidence on the 'risk criteria' and the concerns that might arise in the event of a patient leaving hospital. Equally, an inpatient nurse will probably be well placed to comment on the current degree of mental disorder and any current risk concerns.

The initial questioning of the RC will tend to follow the relevant section in the MHA dealing with Tribunal powers. The summary grid below is from s.72 (Tribunal powers in respect of patients under s.2, s.3, CTOs or Guardianship), which will be the cases most familiar to readers (see Chapter 3).

In many cases, the Judge will hand over to the Medical Member for more detailed questions on the criteria, diagnoses, treatment issues, etc. Judges vary on how many initial questions they may ask before passing on to the Medical Member. The Panel tries to avoid repeating questions that have already been asked, but they may ask a question to elicit further information or to seek clarity on a point.

Likely initial questions of the RC in a s.2 hearing

- Is the patient suffering from a mental disorder?

- Is that disorder of a nature and/or degree that warrants detention in hospital for assessment or assessment followed by treatment for at least a limited period?

- Is detention justified in the interests of the patient's health or safety or for the protection of others? (This is sometimes referred to as the 'risk criteria'.)

These questions are dealing with the legal criteria for s.2 cases (see Chapter 6 for more detail).

Most Medical Members will wish to deal with the statutory criteria in more detail and will probably wish to know what are the current signs, symptoms and manifestations of the mental disorder (degree) and the history and prognosis of the disorder (nature), and may want to hear more detail about the specific concerns the RC has for the patient's health, their safety or for the protection of others if they are discharged from detention.

In this s.2 case, likely follow-up questions might include, *'what is still being assessed?'* and *'how long might that take?'*. The RC might be asked to give a view about the diagnosis; whether this is a confirmed or a working diagnosis; the likely treatment plan and the RCs views of why this could not take place if the patient were discharged from detention.

It is not possible to anticipate every question that might be asked by the Panel and, as we saw in Chapter 3, there are differences in the legal criteria for each section. Sometimes additional questions will arise as the patient speaks or as one witness gives evidence leading to more questions for another witness. In most cases the RC can expect questions about:

- Compliance or non-compliance with treatment;

- Engagement with professionals or therapies;

- Insight;

- Capacity;

- Section 17 leave status and how this is going;

- The detail of any risk incidents.

Once the Medical Member has finished the Specialist Lay Member might ask any follow-up questions. The Chair might then ask any follow-up questions after the other Panel Members have finished. Again, there is no defined structure to this process and the sequence of events may vary from case to case.

Where the patient is an inpatient, the next professional to be questioned will usually be the inpatient nurse. However, in some circumstances, where it is clear at the outset that discharge arrangements are key to the evidence, the author of the social circumstances report may give evidence next.

Questioning of the inpatient nurse could be led by the Specialist Lay Member or the Medical Member and will usually look at the headings as set out in the Practice Direction (PD) and in the report.

Questions will usually include how the patient is progressing on the ward, their understanding of and consent, or not, to treatment for their mental disorder, whether they have any s.17 leave and how this is progressing and any situations where they have gone absent without leave or presented any other management difficulties. Additional questions might include whether they have required any additional PRN ('pro re nata' or as required) medication; any visits from family, friends, etc. and whether the patient is engaged with other treatments on the ward such as nursing care and psychological and occupational therapies.

Nursing evidence usually deals with the current, day-to-day situation for the patient and whether treatment and care might be manageable on an informal basis rather than under MHA powers.

FAQ: What if I don't agree with the RC?

Answer: Nursing staff and care coordinators do not necessarily need to agree with the RC's views or with each other. However, where there is a difference of opinion, it is obviously better for this to be discussed ahead of the hearing. Every professional is entitled to hold different views from their own professional perspective. It is important that witnesses are able to give their own view and reasoning whether or not all are agreed.

The author of the social circumstances report usually goes last and the questioning will usually be led by the Specialist Lay Member.

These questions will tend to follow the PD and might specifically include a request for details of any discharge plan should the patient be discharged from section, the views of the Nearest Relative (NR) and the community support available to the patient.

The author of the SCR should usually be the Care Coordinator or someone with appropriate knowledge of the patient and community resources. Section 117 aftercare plans will be important.

In some cases, the evidence of the author of the social circumstances report will be central to whether or not a patient might be discharged from section.

It is less useful to the Panel when any of the reports are given by someone who either does not know the patient well or has never met them. These situations do occur and mean that the Tribunal may have to ask further questions of other witnesses. In some circumstances it might well be that the absence of a key witness with knowledge of the patient means the hearing is adjourned and those absent are directed to attend the next hearing.

Such a delay in the process can be upsetting to the patient, who may be anxious to have their case heard, and inconvenient to those who did attend.

FAQ: What should I do when I have been instructed to attend a Tribunal for a patient I do not know?

Answer: If you have been told to attend a Tribunal because the author of the report is not available or you have had to prepare a report at short notice, explain the circumstances to the Tribunal. Sometimes this can happen when the patient has just been referred to the team or has recently moved into the area, or the usual Care Coordinator has left or is on leave.

The Tribunal should understand that in these circumstances you may not be able to provide much further detailed evidence.

If you find yourself in this sort of circumstance, you should endeavour to meet with the patient at least briefly; try to discuss the case with any colleagues who do know the patient and read as much of the progress notes and other reports that time allows.

EXPERT QUOTE

If you are asked to give evidence at a Tribunal on behalf of another person at the last minute make sure you do the right thing by the patient and the Tribunal. Read the report that your colleague has prepared, go through notes from the date of the report to the date of the Tribunal and have the decency to meet with the patient, if only for a few minutes. I cannot speak for all Judges but I would always grant time for these three things to be done rather than have someone give evidence who has not read the report, has no background knowledge and has never met the patient.

If the patient gave their evidence at the beginning of the hearing, they will usually be given a final opportunity to respond to the evidence and have the last word should they wish before the hearing concludes.

FAQ: What if I want to speak but have already had my turn?

Answer: In situations where you forgot to mention something or wish to respond to something, do not interrupt someone else's evidence but raise your hand or otherwise indicate to a Panel Member and at an appropriate point the Judge will ask you what you wish to say. You may need to wait until the end of someone else's evidence to speak. If you do make additional points, the patient's representative will be able to direct further questions to you or others on that basis. The Judge will usually ask the representative if there are 'any questions arising' from your additional evidence.

The legal representative: Cross-examination and submissions

If the patient is represented then, in most hearings, the representative will be given the opportunity to 'cross-examine' the professionals once the Tribunal Members have asked their questions. Cross-examination simply means questions to a person who has already given their main evidence. There is no rule about the order of this, and on occasion Judges might ask the representative to lead on the questioning of a professional before the Panel ask their questions. This might happen if, for example, the patient is seeking something very specific such as a recommendation for leave or transfer.

It might be helpful to readers to have an understanding of the representative's agenda and what they will have done in preparation for the hearing as lines of questioning might appear odd or clinically inappropriate to professionals. In simple terms, the representative's role is to try to apply the law to the patient's instructions ('instructions' simply being what the patient wants and what the patient says about a particular matter such as diagnosis or an alleged incident) and to act in their best legal interests.

The Law Society's guidance for representatives states:

> *If you conclude that your client has the capacity to instruct you, you must take instructions from them and act in accordance with those instructions, even where they are inconsistent, unhelpful to the case or vary during the preparation of the case, or during the hearing itself.*

> *(The Law Society: Representation before Mental Health Tribunals. Practice Note 2019)*

For a patient in the midst of a relapse of their mental disorder, one can imagine that their instructions might be completely at odds with professional opinion, but nevertheless the representative has a duty to advance arguments in support of the patient's position if they are properly arguable and the Law Society guidance further states:

> *It is highly unlikely that to seek a client's discharge in accordance with his or her express wishes would not be 'properly arguable', even if it is unlikely to succeed ... your duty to act in accordance with the client's instructions takes precedence over your duty to act in what you perceive to be their best clinical interests.*

> *(Ibid.)*

In preparation for the hearing, as well as carefully considering the reports, the representative should also have read the medical and nursing notes and the section papers and is very likely to ask questions about any inconsistencies or differences of opinion. This is one of several reasons why it is important for professionals to read colleagues' reports as well as their own in preparation for the hearing. If the patient is seeking discharge then the representative will, of course, be trying to demonstrate to the Panel that at least one of the criteria for detention or community compulsion are no longer met (see Chapter 6 for the specific legal criteria for each type of case). The representative may also be trying to construct a less restrictive alternative to detention in hospital for the patient's treatment and care so you can imagine that questions might focus on previous periods of informal treatment or successful community follow-up. There may be incidents described in the reports that the patient has specifically instructed the representative to challenge.

In NR application cases, both the patient and the NR may be represented and therefore there may be two stages of cross-examination.

At the end of the hearing the patient's representative will usually be given the opportunity to make their 'submissions' (sometimes referred to as 'summing up') confirming what the Tribunal is being asked to do (for example, discharge the patient from detention) and highlighting any aspects of the evidence that support the patient's case. In many cases, the issues will have become very clear in the course of the evidence and submissions might be brief.

Deliberations and the decision

At the end of the hearing, the Judge will then ask all to leave and the Panel will be left to deliberate in private on the evidence that has been heard. The duration of these deliberations will depend on the complexity of the case or how finely balanced the issues are.

Once the Panel has completed their deliberations, at least one representative of the Responsible Authority (RC, nurse or MHA Administrator) will be required to attend to hear the verbal decision and in most cases the patient and their representative will also attend. If there are concerns about how the patient might react to a negative outcome, the decision might be given by a Panel Member or the representative on the ward rather than in the less contained environment of the hearing room.

> ### EXPERT QUOTE
>
> *Always return to the Tribunal to hear the decision. Often, the Tribunal will offer words of support or guidance to the patient, and these may offer you a platform to continue to work and engage with your patient in the future.*

Nearest Relative applications

The usual process for proceedings will be much as described with the exception that it is the NR who is applying for the patient's discharge. They would only be able to do so in certain circumstances and additional criteria might apply. For example, if they had ordered the discharge of certain patients and been 'barred' by the RC (s.23 and s.25 MHA), they would be able to apply to the Tribunal. The additional grounds for the Tribunal to consider would include the 'dangerousness test' set out in s.72(1)(b)(iii) that the patient, if released, would be likely to act in a manner dangerous to other persons or to himself (see Chapter 6).

The NR could also have their own legal representation alongside the patient. The NR will have the opportunity to give evidence and their representative may cross-examine witnesses.

Top tips

It may go without saying for most people who are reading this book, but it is worth reminding readers that their conduct is important when attending hearings. The best way to approach preparations for attending the Tribunal is to prepare as you would for any other Court hearing. In summary:

- *Appropriate dress (not, for example, cycle shorts, which is a real example).*

- *Arriving on time.*

- *No drinks or chewing gum.*

- *No texting or emailing on mobile devices.*

- *Being well prepared for questioning and cross-examination on the evidence you provide.*

- *Understanding that this is not a case conference or ward round where professionals can interrupt and debate.*

- *Understanding that there are rules for taking evidence and any wish to make a specific point will need to be asked via the Judge at an appropriate point in the proceedings.*

- *Ensuring that you have read the other reports and have discussed any differences of opinion ahead of the proceedings.*

- *Address the Panel and not your colleagues or patient when giving your evidence and answering questions of the Panel.*

- *Address the patient's representative when answering their questions.*

- *Do not send an ill-prepared junior member of staff on your behalf.*

- *Most of the guidance in Chapter 7 on written evidence can also be applied to oral evidence.*

- *The best way to plan for questioning and cross-examination is to review the headings in the relevant section of the PDs and be able to answer questions on each.*

- *It is helpful to have the relevant criteria clear in your mind as these will be underlying most of the questions from the Panel and the representative.*

- *Focus on the question that has been asked.*

Chapter summary

This chapter has looked at:

- The usual venue for hearings.

- Whether the hearing is private or public.

- Practicalities (who is in attendance and what happens before the actual hearing takes place).

- Preliminary matters (issues that might need resolution ahead of the hearing).

- Proceedings – who goes first and how the Tribunal manage the hearing.

- Usual seating plan.

- Likely questions that would be asked.

Chapter 10
The welfare of the patient

Introduction

This chapter provides guidance and tips for professionals on assisting and supporting patients throughout the Tribunal proceedings.

Everyone involved in Tribunal proceedings should ensure that the 'voice' of the patient is central to the proceedings. We provide some prompts throughout this chapter for how this can be best achieved.

We acknowledge that there are no direct quotations from patients (for reasons of confidentiality and ethics). However, we would advise professionals to ask the patient in advance of the Tribunal how they can assist and enable them to feel as at ease as possible. Each patient's experience of Tribunals will be unique as are their individual needs. However, there are some common themes, some of which are discussed in other chapters but are reiterated here. For example, did you meet with the patient in advance of the hearing, share your report with them, ensure they were given adequate information about the Tribunal and avoid contributing to delays by submitting your reports on time? If you are the Responsible Clinician (RC), did you consider whether the relevant statutory criteria continue to be met or whether the patient should be discharged ahead of the Tribunal?

> *EXPERT QUOTE*
>
> *Make sure you have explained your report, or at the very least, your conclusions to your patient. This way, the patient is not surprised in the hearing, and will already be aware of your opinion.*

The patients' experience

For many patients, an application to the Tribunal will be their best chance of discharge in the face of professional opposition. Even if professionals do not agree with the patient about their readiness for discharge from detention, patients are likely to need their help with the process. A supportive team will offer adequate assistance and encouragement to patients who are seeking to apply to the Tribunal.

Some Tribunal hearings will arise because of an automatic reference rather than a patient's application (as we saw in Chapter 2). The patient might decide not to attend a hearing they have not asked for. However, many of the points in this chapter should be of use in all cases.

As we have seen, although the discharge rates at most Tribunal hearings are relatively low, there may be other advantages to the patient from having a Tribunal. In 2011, the Care Quality Commission and Administrative Justice and Tribunals Council published Patients Experiences of the First-tier Tribunal (Mental Health). The report indicated that the Tribunal:

is an important safeguard for patients, not only as a means of challenging their detention, but also in finding out about and measuring their progress and in check-ing whether care plans are appropriate and meeting their needs.

In other words, from the patient's perspective, there may be benefit to the process if not the outcome.

This report aimed to look at the direct experience of patients in England via satisfaction surveys. There has been no further such research report since 2011 although the Care Quality Commission (CQC) and Health Inspectorate Wales (HIW) annual reports on the use of the Mental Health Act (MHA) do sometimes make reference to various aspects of the Tribunal.

Some of the points raised in the 2011 report above are now out-of-date, but many remain relevant today, including:

- *Delays from application to hearing dates caused anxiety for patients.*

- *There was a range of positive and negative experiences of the Tribunal process by patients.*

- *The hospital should not recommend lawyers to a patient as it might give the appearance of bias (as they are the 'opposing party').*

- *Hospital staff as well as the Medical Member of the Tribunal and the legal representative should explain the purpose of any pre-hearing examination (PHE) to the patient, and the PHE should not take place on the day of the hearing as this adds stress to for patient.*

- *Hospital Managers should give patients information about what will happen at the Tribunal.*

- *Reports should be provided in good time and copies sent to the patient and their representative well before the hearing (note the report indicated that nearly a third of patients believed they had never seen any of the reports in advance of the hearing).*

- *The venue should be soundproof, properly air-conditioned, with waiting areas for patients and their representatives.*

- *The order of proceedings should take account of any wishes expressed by the patient.*

- *Patients should be put at their ease.*

- *The Tribunal decision should be given verbally and a written copy sent as soon as possible to the hospital and patient.*

Bartlett and Sandland (2013, pp533–34) refer to a small survey in which:

> *patients were often dissatisfied with Tribunals, irrespective of whether they were formal or informal in procedural terms. The main problems identified ... were that Tribunal hearings were alienating experiences, and Tribunal Members were often (at least seemingly) uninterested in the patients' side of the story, with patients given little opportunity to speak ...*

The CQC and HIW have indicated within various annual reports on the use of the MHA that they have had to provide information to patients on their rights to apply to the Tribunal when they appeared to be unaware of their rights, that sometimes they were not made aware of their rights in a timely manner in order to apply to the Tribunal and that in some cases, the RC discharged the patients *'in the 48 hours before the hearings for patients on s.3, 37 or Community Treatment Orders'* (see CQC: Monitoring the Mental Health Act 2016/17). They make the point that such experiences raise anxiety levels for the patient when it may have been possible to provide information or discharge in a more timely manner.

There are various research papers setting out the limitations and inadequacies of aspects of the Tribunal from various perspectives. We do not attempt to set the arguments out here. However, it is clear that the requirements to involve patients, put them at their ease and explain the process applies equally to the Tribunal Panel Members as it does to all other professionals.

Anecdotally, we are aware of patients considering withdrawing their application as a result of pressure from professionals and/or family, worrying about how the RC or Care Coordinator will respond, feeling that the Tribunal puts them 'on trial' or that they have committed an offence or some wrongdoing when they have not. Attending a Tribunal can be a stressful and intimidating experience for those who are expected to sit and listen to others discussing their life and mental health history. When the person's liberty is at stake, this elevates the potential for patients to perceive inequity and powerlessness.

Given this background, everyone with various duties and responsibilities to the Tribunal should take a proactive approach to minimise any negative experiences. These are set out below in the form of a checklist.

Access to relevant information and support about the Tribunal process

Have the relevant Hospital Managers or Local Authority ensured that the patient understands what their rights are to apply to the Tribunal and have they given this information in an accessible format?

Are patients aware of when their case might be automatically referred to the Tribunal?

Note the points above in practice are likely to be undertaken both by the MHA Administration team and inpatient nursing staff at the relevant hospital. For patients subject to Community Treatment Orders (CTOs), Guardianship or conditional discharge, it might be a Care Coordinator or member of a community team (s.132(1)(b) and s.132A MHA and Code 20.34 (W), 20.31(E)).

In the relevant circumstances is there a process for requesting a discretionary reference to the Tribunal by the Secretary of State?

Has an Independent Mental Health Advocate (IMHA) been made available to the patient? The IMHA has a duty to assist the patient to obtain and understand their rights under the MHA and how to exercise these rights. Note that the MHA Codes (4.23(E), 37.17 (W)) state that if the patient lacks capacity to decide whether to seek a review of detention or a CTO, an IMHA should be introduced to them so that they can explain what help they can offer. The IMHA holds a unique and specific role to assist the patient before, during and after a Tribunal.

Have the staff team ensured they encourage patients to understand and exercise their rights?

Do staff teams ensure that they do not actively discourage patients from doing so? Many staff will have heard patients voice reluctance to apply to the Tribunal for fear of affecting relationships with the team or of other negative consequences. Professionals should be mindful that the patient has a right to appeal against their section even when the professional team might feel this course of action would be unhelpful to the patient's care and treatment.

Are patients offered specific assistance to make an application to the Tribunal when they voice a wish to do so? Note the MHA Code (Para 4.22(E) and 4.25(W)) states that Hospital Managers should ensure patients are offered assistance to make an application and that the application is transmitted without delay. The same applies to Local Authorities for Guardianship cases.

Is there a checklist for ensuring that patients are told the following?

- How to contact a suitably qualified legal representative (and be given assistance to do so if required);

- That representation for Tribunal proceedings will be free;

- How to contact any other organisation that may be able to help them make an application to the Tribunal.

In practice, patients should be able to submit an application relatively easily, either by themselves or via ward staff, community staff, IMHA or their legal representative. Are you aware of how to assist a patient with this? Where are the forms, and how would these be sent on to the Tribunal Office? Is there an internal form that is sent to the MHA Administration team? Who completes the formal application?

All professionals should be aware of the role of the legal representative in assisting the patient with their application.

Does your hospital or unit enable visits from legal representatives at any reasonable time? (Code 12.7(W) and 12.8(E)). Legal representatives have their own duties to act in the best interests of their client.

If a patient is not represented, professionals and the Tribunal should be particularly mindful of supporting the patient sufficiently and the overriding objective of the Tribunal to deal with the case fairly and justly. An unrepresented patient may require further assistance from the Panel to give their evidence and to ensure questioning of the professionals is focused and relevant. See Chapter 9 for more details of legal representation for patients.

The Tribunal in England will send out an information for patients leaflet either directly to the patient, or via their legal representative if they have one, to advise patients of their rights to legal representation and to see the Tribunal doctor in advance of the hearing.

The information for patients leaflets can be found at:

www.gov.uk.government/publications/mental-health-review-Tribunal-information-for-patients-t121-andt122

The MHRTW has a range of guidance booklets for patients on its website at:

www.mentalhealthreviewtribunal.gov.wales

Specific requirements and reasonable adjustments at the hearing

As we saw in Chapter 7, the English and Welsh Practice Directions (PDs) for reports ask the Responsible Authority to set out information in advance to assist with the Tribunal's duties under the Equality Act 2010. This includes:

- *whether the patient suffers from any disability requiring assistance to take part;*
- *whether an interpreter is required for the patient's first language/dialect;*
- *if deaf, whether British Sign Language interpreters or a relay interpreter is required.*

This means that any adjustments can be made in advance of the hearing by the Tribunal.

Patients must not be at any disadvantage as a result of their mental disorder, age, gender, sexual orientation, race, religion or marital status. If any additional aids or adaptations or adjustments are needed, everyone has a responsibility to raise that ahead of the hearing wherever possible.

It is important that patients are able to understand and participate in the hearing. Hospital Managers and Local Authorities (in Guardianship cases) should inform the Tribunal 'well in advance' if they think such services might be necessary (Code 12.40 (E), 12.30 (W)). The MHRTW has a Welsh-language scheme and hearings can be held in either English or Welsh depending on the patient's language of choice (Code 12.28 (W)).

Following on from this, in most cases, the PD requires professionals to identify:

any factors that might affect the patient's understanding or ability to cope with the hearing and whether there are any adjustments that the Tribunal may consider in order to deal with the case fairly and justly.

Professionals will usually know the patient much better than the legal representative or the Panel. They should therefore not feel inhibited in letting the Panel or representative know if anything more can be done to ensure the patient's rights and needs are met in relation to the Tribunal.

This includes adjustments on the day, such as when the patient gives their evidence, where they may want to sit, whether they wish anyone to be with them, whether they have cognitive or other difficulties affecting their understanding of the process. This can include simply explaining that in your professional judgement the patient might not manage to sit throughout the full hearing or that they may need regular breaks. Basically, think about how you can assist the Panel to ensure a fair hearing.

The environment

It is understood that many venues have to make use of what is available on-site. That might be a room that is also used as an art therapy or occupational therapy room or a ward round/ conference room. However, it should still be made suitable for the purposes of a Tribunal hearing.

Have you ensured that the Tribunal will take place in an environment that is not intimidating? (Code 20.34 (W), 2031(E)). For example, is the room adequate to avoid over-crowding and is seating of a similar height for all participants (e.g. patients or staff are not seated lower than Panel Members)?

Is the room private, clean and adequately sized and furnished, containing no confidential information about other patients? Is it safe from potential hazards and is there an alarm system? We will also look later at safety issues when hearings take place on a ward.

For CTO, Guardianship or conditionally discharged patients, have you considered that a hospital setting may not be the most appropriate? Is there a suitable community setting?

Concerns over the safety of the patient or others

Any concerns over the safety of the patient or others should be made clear to the Panel ahead of the hearing where possible. A range of pre-emptive actions can be taken if risk issues are raised in advance. If the patient is too unwell to attend a hearing room, the hearing might take place on the ward, in liaison with the Panel and the Hospital Managers. The Tribunal Panel can also exclude any person who may disrupt proceedings. The patient can bring a friend, relative or IMHA with them for support and can attend the start of the hearing then leave. The patient should be permitted to have reasonable breaks if needed during the hearing.

If nursing staff or others are concerned about the patient's likely distress during proceedings, they should set this out in the relevant paragraph of their report and alert the Panel before the hearing starts. The patient can also explain directly or via their representative if they have a specific wish or requirement during the proceedings.

Practicalities such as whether or not a patient is allowed to bring drinks into the hearing, or items to show as evidence, will be for the Tribunal Panel to decide.

The Tribunal Panel will ensure appropriate seating arrangements and they are aware that patients may be unwell and that the proceedings might exacerbate certain symptoms or stress levels. Thus, the requirement for the Tribunal to be relatively informal and flexible in approach whilst keeping in mind the seriousness of the proceedings.

Nursing staff may have to manage a hearing in a ward environment in some situations. They are entitled to expect Panel Members to adhere to their safety and security requirements such as the removal of ties. However, many Judges now use laptops to take notes and will require access to the equipment inside the hearing room. All of this should be agreed in advance so that the issue does not cause delay and consequently increase anxiety for the patient.

Assistance at the pre-hearing examination (PHE) stage and in preparation for the hearing

The CQC research mentioned earlier suggested that many patients were not clear about the reason for any PHE, that many times the examination took place on the day of the Tribunal, potentially exacerbating anxiety and that the actual examinations were inconsistent in approach. Furthermore, many patients had not realised that the outcome of the PHE would be fed back at the hearing to the Panel and professionals and that it would contribute towards the Panel's decision whether to discharge or not.

It is inevitable that PHEs may vary in approach, depending on the section and the patients' presentation at the time of the examination. However, the legal representative, the Hospital Managers or Local Authority and, indeed, the Medical Member should make it clear to the patient what the purpose of the PHE is.

Information on the PHE is available on the MHRTW website and in the English Tribunal information sheet setting out the purposes of the PHE, how the information will be used, when and where the interview takes place and how the doctor feeds back the information from the examination to the Panel and to the hearing.

Attending the hearing and ensuring the patient's involvement

Those giving evidence to the Tribunal:

> *Should do what they can to help enable hearings to be conducted in a professional manner, which includes having regard to the patient's wishes and feelings and ensuring that the patient feels as comfortable with the proceedings as possible.*

> *(Code Para 12.4 (E and W))*

There are some specific Tribunal Rules about the welfare of the patient as well as some common-sense practice points explained below.

Where the patient has a legal representative, it is their job to assist in managing the process, assist the patient to give their evidence, cross-examine witnesses, with an eye to the need to avoid an adversarial approach that might impact on relationships between the patient and the professionals. Training courses for mental health lawyers will usually emphasise that it is incumbent on the legal representative to leave relationships between the patient and the treating team as intact as they were at the start of the Tribunal proceedings.

The patient's representative will be able to advise when the patient would like to speak although ultimately the order of evidence is a matter for the Tribunal to decide. Some patients like to hear all the evidence and speak last and others prefer to go first then leave. Whatever the order of evidence, most Panels will ensure the patient has an opportunity to speak to them again at the end of the hearing.

It can, of course, be intimidating and for this reason the patient's representative will usually ask questions of the patient to try and set out their case, deal with any points that have arisen during the hearing and to keep the patient's evidence focused as far as possible on the legal criteria being considered by the Panel.

Panel Members can also ask the patient questions, but these should be relevant to the proceedings. In some cases, where the representative has set out the patient's case clearly, the Panel Members may have less to ask the patient.

ACTIVITY *10.1*

Research has stated that patients can feel intimidated by the Tribunal process and that their views are not given equal weight by those in attendance. Consider the following question and note down your thoughts.

Question:

- *How can professionals ensure patients are heard and that they are made to feel at ease?*

Although we have seen in Chapter 7 that the PDs state that authors 'should have personally met and be familiar with the patient' it is understood that there are going to be circumstances where an attendee has not met with the patient, is unfamiliar with their case or is not the author of the report. All of this might disadvantage the patient unless the parties seek to ensure the patient is as involved and updated as possible.

In these instances, check that the report follows the relevant PD, submit the report in adequate time, giving patients and their representatives sufficient chance to peruse the report. This should contribute to a hearing that is less stressful for the patient as well as others. In all instances, attendees should:

- Introduce themselves to the patient ahead of the hearing;

- Familiarise oneself with the contents of all reports;

- Ensure they are in a position to update the Panel and answer any questions from the report;

- Ensure your reports do not ignore the heading requirements referring to *strengths or positive factors* relating to the patient, and in social circumstances reports to report the patient's *'views, wishes, beliefs, opinions, hopes and concerns'*.

If, for any reason, any of these steps are not possible, be honest and explain in the report and at the hearing what steps you took and why any step was not possible. We are aware of professionals being asked to write reports the day after returning from leave, or to attend hearings with a morning's notice. Professionals may also have other crisis-work or situations to deal with on any given day.

Tribunal Panel Members are human beings and do understand when individuals are placed in difficult positions. The most important thing to bear in mind is that this is a Tribunal about a patient, not about you, and that patient should not be disadvantaged as a result of any of the above.

This is why, in part, the additional requirements in the PD refer to the patient's strengths, their wishes, beliefs, hopes and concerns with the expectation that those providing written and oral evidence can, as a minimum, understand the issues from the patient's perspective.

Concerns over giving evidence in front of the patient

Professionals sometimes report that they feel the Tribunal was damaging to the relationship they had with the patient. They do not like having to make comments on the patients' mental disorder or presentation, in particular where they are aware the patient disagrees with them.

In many cases, where the professionals have met with the patient ahead of the hearing and have ensured the patient has sight of their report in plenty of time, they can usually explain and again acknowledge in the hearing that there may be differences of opinion. Professionals should remember that the legal representative will go through the reports with the patient anyway so there is nothing to be gained from avoiding discussing the reports and an initial explanation of the report contents from the author is likely to be much more beneficial to the patient.

Information at the hearing should not come as a surprise to the patient if they are in communication with the professional as part of their regular care and treatment or community follow-up. In our experience, patients are much more able to tolerate information or opinion they disagree with at a hearing if they were already aware of it.

Anecdotally, some patients have stated to the authors that they liked hearing the professionals being cross-examined and questioned and having to explain their position to an independent Panel.

It is perfectly acceptable at a hearing to say that you are aware of differences of opinion over views. There is no need to risk humiliating or destroying the relationship with the patient. The Panel should also be sensitive to this.

We are aware that sometimes, in an attempt to show sensitivity and collaboration with the patient, professionals might aim their answers or discussion at the patient rather than Panel Members. It is likely the Judge will remind them that this is not a case conference and that they should address the Panel and not the patient. This is why, where possible, those discussions should take place with the patient ahead of the hearing.

EXPERT QUOTE

A number of report writers are concerned about the therapeutic relationship between themselves and the patient, which is why they do not form a final conclusion. It is easier for the patient if they know of the author's view before the Tribunal (especially if the author has taken time to go through the report with the patient) rather than hearing it for the first time at the Tribunal.

ACTIVITY 10.2

Imagine attending your own Tribunal and listening to a range of information about your life and circumstances and professionals' views on your current situation.

Questions:

- *How would you manage the process and what would assist you?*

- *What would you do and how might you feel if you disagreed or felt the situation to be unfair?*

Enabling others to attend to support the patient

The patient should be enabled to have someone of their choice attend the Tribunal with them and assist them ahead of the hearing. This may be the Nearest Relative (NR) or another relative or friend. In many situations an IMHA will also attend and provide additional support to the patient.

The final decision on whether any person should be given permission to attend rests with the Tribunal. The Tribunal will usually want to assist the patient and enable anyone who could support them to attend. However, there are instances in which the Tribunal might set limits on when and how they attend and whether they wish to hear directly from the person. First, they will want to know what their role is to be: are they there to support or to give evidence? Do they understand the role of the Tribunal? Are there any safeguarding concerns about this persons' attendance?

See Chapter 5 for more details on who can attend the hearing.

Patients who do not attend the hearing

The MHA Code (Para 12.28 (E) and 12.31 (W)) states that patients and carers do not need to attend the Tribunal hearing, but professionals should encourage and support them to attend unless they judge that it would be detrimental to the patient's health or wellbeing.

However, note that whether or not professionals are of the view that it would be detrimental to the patient, the decision of whether or not a person can attend rests with the Tribunal. The Tribunal will never compel a patient to attend and may proceed without the patient as long they are satisfied the patient knew about the hearing and the Tribunal Rules have been complied with.

ACTIVITY 10.3

Trude has a long-awaited Tribunal hearing this afternoon and has now told her representative and the ward staff that she has no intention of attending.

Question:

- *What should the representative and ward staff do now? Does it harm Trude's case if she does not attend?*

Support after the hearing

The decision is usually given verbally by the Tribunal on the day of the hearing (see Chapters 9 and 11). This might be directly to the patient or relayed to them by the hospital staff or legal representative. Legal representatives will usually then explain the decision to the patient and go through the details of the written decision with the patient at a later date.

Where the patient has been unsuccessful in gaining the outcome they wanted, this is often an opportunity for staff to discuss future plans and goals. It is certainly a time where the patient should be offered support and reassurance rather than informed that staff were right all along!

Further resources

Many voluntary organisations have helpful material for patients on the Tribunal process. Patients may prefer information that is not directly associated with the Tribunal or Responsible Authority. For example, Young Minds has some helpful leaflets at:

https://youngminds.org.uk/media/2779/youngminds_guide-to-mental-health_v3.pdf

And Mind also have helpful information for adults at:

www.mind.org.uk/information-support/legal-rights/leaving-hospital/mental-health-Tribunal/

There is also a helpful *Guide to Mental Health Tribunals for Young People* written by the Royal College of Psychiatrists and the Tribunals Judiciary in 2016. This can be found at:

www.rcpsych.ac.uk/docs/default-source/members/faculties/child-and-adolescent-psychiatry/cap-camhs-guide-to-mental-health-Tribunals-feb-2016.pdf?sfvrsn=cf42b347_2

Top tips

- *Don't forget that patients have a legal right to a hearing, whether or not their treating team agree with them.*

- *Make sure patients are aware of their rights to apply to the Tribunal.*

- *Ensure any IMHAs visiting detained or community patients are also made aware of new patients who may need their rights explained and opportunities to discuss applying to the Tribunal.*

- *Hospital Managers, Local Authorities and all attendees at the hearing should ensure that the patient is put at their ease and assisted to participate fully.*

- *Don't forget that patients might find the Tribunal process helpful even if they do not 'win'.*

Chapter summary

- Hospital Managers, Local Authorities and the Tribunal are required to give patients adequate information on their right to appeal and on the appeal process.

- Information should be in an accessible format and easy to understand.

- Patients should be able to ask questions and gain specific assistance from a legal representative and IMHA as well as support and advice from their hospital or community teams.

- Patients are entitled to any support or additional services that ensure their equal participation in Tribunals.

- Specific lawyers should not be recommended by hospitals or Local Authorities as it gives the impression of bias. They can offer a list of accredited representatives.

- Patients should be put at their ease by everyone involved in the hearing process.

- The patient's viewpoint and perspective should be given equal weight to that of the treating team.

Chapter 11

Decisions, reviews and appeals

Disagreements and complaints

Introduction

This chapter will cover the legal requirements and the practicalities of how Tribunal decisions are given to the parties and will briefly cover the legal and procedural matters that can arise *after* the conclusion of a Tribunal hearing. The chapter will also cover amendment of minor errors, getting a decision set aside, seeking a review of a decision, appeals against a decision because of an error of law and complaints.

For professionals, in the vast majority of cases, Tribunals end once the verbal decision has been given on the day of the hearing and everyone moves on to their next piece of work – unless, of course, the patient has been discharged from detention by the Tribunal and urgent work is required to arrange community follow-up or aftercare.

Appeals against Tribunal decisions are relatively rare and it is particularly rare for NHS Trusts or Health Boards to pursue appeals against Tribunal decisions – it is much more likely that the detained patient will wish to pursue any possibility of overturning a decision that has gone against them, resulting in their continued detention. If an appeal is submitted then it is likely that the matter will be dealt with by the hospital's legal department; however, professionals may be asked to provide statements or information relevant to the case.

If you recall the diagram of the Court system in Chapter 1, we have a hierarchy of Courts in England and Wales and, in all areas of law, an appeal against a Court's decision is to the next Court up in the hierarchy. So, in mental health cases, an appeal against a Tribunal decision is first made to the Upper Tribunal (which has taken over most of the functions of the High Court as far as mental health cases are concerned). An appeal against an Upper Tribunal decision is to the Court of Appeal and an appeal against a Court of Appeal decision is to the Supreme Court, which is the most senior domestic Court. Any challenge to a Supreme Court decision could only then be to the European Court of Human Rights (ECtHR) if all domestic remedies have been exhausted and there is a human rights aspect to the case.

Here is an example of a case that travelled all the way up through the domestic Court hierarchy even though the patient was discharged from their Community Treatment Order (CTO) a few months after the initial Tribunal hearing:

Welsh Ministers v PJ *[2018] UKSC 66*

PJ was a gentleman in his 40s with diagnoses of mild learning disability and an autism spectrum disorder. He had spent most of his adult life in hospital settings and had a forensic history, including ABH and threats to kill. PJ was discharged from hospital to a care home under a CTO in September 2011. The placement at the care home included extensive risk mitigation measures and PJ's 'leave' from the home was, in the main, escorted, he remained under observations every 15 minutes, was only permitted a minimal amount of alcohol and would be restrained as a last resort if he sought to leave the home.

A Tribunal hearing took place in May 2014. PJ sought discharge from the CTO, primarily because he wished to have more freedom to see his family and girlfriend. It was argued on PJ's behalf that his access to the community was being restricted and he was subject to an unlawful deprivation of liberty and therefore the Tribunal should use their discretion to discharge the CTO and bring the unlawful deprivation of liberty to an end. The Tribunal decided first that the regime was not a deprivation of liberty and, even if it was, the need for the CTO took precedence over PJ's human rights.

Unsurprisingly, PJ (via his legal representatives) appealed to the Upper Tribunal. At this stage, the dispute was between PJ and the Health Board responsible for the CTO. The Upper Tribunal added the Secretary of State for Health and the Welsh Ministers as parties to the case because of the important legal principles raised by the case. Both declined to participate and even applied to be removed as parties (unsuccessfully). The Upper Tribunal decided that PJ was probably deprived of his liberty, the CTO did not take precedence over his human rights and a Tribunal faced with an unlawful deprivation of liberty could not allow it to continue.

Rather oddly, given the Welsh Ministers previously neutral stance and previous application to be removed as a party, they appealed to the Court of Appeal and the case was heard in March 2017. This is why in the later cases in this saga the name of the case changes from 'PJ v A Local Health Board' to 'Welsh Ministers v PJ'.

As is often the case, as legal proceedings progress, the arguments had narrowed and crystallised and, by this stage, the case was really only about whether a Responsible Clinician (RC) could impose conditions under a CTO that amount to an objective deprivation of liberty. The Court of Appeal decided that an RC does have the power to do this as long as the restrictions are less than those that existed when the patient was in hospital. They also decided that the Tribunal had no power to discharge a patient because of a human rights breach.

PJ then appealed to the Supreme Court who heard the case in October 2018 and decided there was nothing in the MHA giving an RC the power to impose a deprivation of liberty under a CTO and therefore they could not do so. The Supreme Court did agree with the Court of Appeal that a Tribunal could not discharge a CTO on human rights grounds if the criteria in the MHA (s.72) were met but could advise all concerned about the true legal effect of the CTO.

ACTIVITY 11.1

Having read the case example above, consider the following questions.

- *Can you explain which Court made the final decision and what the decision was?*

- *Is that decision binding on a future Tribunal?*

(You may need to refer back to the Court structure information in Chapter 1.)

Decisions

A Tribunal *may* give a decision orally at a hearing and *must* provide written reasons within three working days of a s.2 hearing and within seven days in all other cases. The written decision must include the decision itself, the reasons for the decision and information regarding rights of appeal (Rule 41 (E), Rule 28 (W)).

> Decisions: '... are not intended to include a comprehensive and detailed analysis of the case, either in terms of fact or in law ... their purpose remains what it has always been, which is to tell the parties in broad terms why they lose or, as the case may be, win'.
>
> (SL v Ludlow Street Healthcare [2015])

The 'lose' or 'win' language in this case is being employed as shorthand. Inquisitorial Tribunal proceedings are an exercise in the independent evaluation of evidence, and an unsuccessful application means that, on balance, the Tribunal have found the legal criteria for detention to be met – not that the patient has 'lost'.

The decision is covered by Rule 14 (Rule 17 in Wales), and therefore a decision could be withheld from a patient if the serious harm test is met (see Chapter 7). This would be highly unusual.

In most cases, once all of the evidence has been heard, the Panel will have a private discussion and then the patient and professionals will be invited back into the hearing to receive the oral decision. Judges vary in how much detail they will go into with an oral decision and may simply confirm whether the patient is to be discharged or not with the detailed explanation for the decision following in the written reasons. If there are concerns about the patient's response to a negative outcome, the Panel may decide to give the decision to the professionals and legal representative and ask that this be communicated to the patient in the more contained environment of the ward.

The written decision will, in practice, be sent by secure email to the MHA Administration team and legal representative or posted directly to the patient if they are unrepresented.

Minor errors

The Tribunal Rules allow for minor mistakes to be simply amended without further formal process. This is sometimes referred to as the 'slip' rule and covers clerical mistakes or accidental slips or omissions. Examples might be misspelt names, mistakes with dates or grammar mistakes. An amended version of the decision will be sent out to the parties if an amendment is made (Rule 44 (E), Rule 29 (W)).

Procedural errors

If there has been a procedural error rather than a legal one – i.e. something in the management of the case has led to unfairness in some way, then an application to set aside and re-make the decision (by holding a new hearing) can be made under the English Rules (Rule 45 (E), there is no equivalent rule in Wales).

The Rules specify the following reasons for seeking a decision to be set aside:

- A document was not sent to or not received by a party or not sent to the Tribunal on time.

- A party or their representative was not present at a hearing.

- Some other procedural irregularity.

It is also possible to challenge a direction of the Tribunal made in the course of the proceedings (see Rule 6(5) (E); there is no equivalent rule in Wales, but this could be dealt with by simply seeking an alternative direction).

Review of a decision

If a party asks for permission to appeal against a decision and there is an obvious error of law then, under the English Rules, the Tribunal can simply review the decision and correct it or set it aside without the need for a potentially lengthy appeal procedure (Rule 47 and 49 (E), there is no equivalent rule in Wales).

Appeals

FAQ: What can I do if I disagree with a Tribunal's decision?

Answer: It is important to note that permission from the Tribunal is required to submit an appeal or, if the Tribunal refuse permission, then the Upper Tribunal can be asked to grant permission. It is also important to remember that a Tribunal decision can only be appealed on the narrow basis that an error of law was made. It is not possible to appeal a decision because you disagree with it – something that can be quite difficult to explain to a patient after an unsuccessful hearing.

In *JLG v Managers of Llanarth Court* [2011] the Upper Tribunal identified the following matters as potential errors of law:

- *Not dealing with the correct legal questions or statutory criteria.*

- *Irrational findings – i.e. findings that no reasonable Tribunal Panel could have made.*

- *Not answering the legal questions appropriately given any findings of fact that were made. The link between any findings of fact and conclusions on the legal questions has to be rational.*

- *Not ensuring a fair hearing for the parties. An example might be if there was a conflict of interest between a Panel Member and one of the professionals or if the Panel declined to consider important evidence.*

- *Reasons for the decision being inadequate. If you go back to the quote from the Ludlow case above then you will see that a decision that failed to explain to the parties why one 'won' and another 'lost' would almost certainly be inadequate.*

Permission to appeal might also be granted if the case raises an important point of law that would be assisted by the Upper Tribunal considering the case – the PJ case described above is a good example of this.

If permission to appeal is granted then all the parties will be notified and given the opportunity to file written responses. A decision might be made on the papers or will progress to an oral hearing. Another possible outcome is that the parties reach agreement, and a consent order is made without the need for any hearing. It would be unusual for professionals to attend an oral appeal hearing as these are arguments over points of law being dealt with by legal representatives in front of an Upper Tribunal Judge.

An application for permission to appeal must be submitted within 28 days of the original decision being sent to the party, and if permission is refused then an application for permission to appeal to the Upper Tribunal must be made within a month of the refusal.

Judicial review of either a Tribunal decision or an Upper Tribunal decision is also a possibility but beyond the scope of this book. For a helpful and detailed summary of the operation of judicial review in mental health cases, see Fennell, Letts and Wilson (2013, pp236–40).

Disagreements

There may be occasions when a Tribunal decision is difficult to understand for the professionals dealing with the patient – perhaps a patient has been discharged despite a high level of clinical concern. It is important to remember that the Tribunal's decision is a legal one not a clinical one and therefore the appropriate mechanisms for the Responsible Authority to challenge a decision would also be to seek a review or appeal as above – perhaps after seeking legal advice from the NHS body or Local Authority. It is also important to say that professionals attending a hearing should not view a decision that goes against their recommendations as some sort of indictment of their assessments, evidence or expertise. As we have seen, Tribunals are 'inquisitorial', and their duty is to evaluate the evidence and apply it to the legal criteria as best they can. Mental health is, by its nature, an uncertain and unpredictable area of work and Tribunal cases tend to rely on judgement and opinion and lack the hard facts you might find in a criminal case, for example. All of this is equally true for the patient, although this is a difficult message to communicate to someone who has been told they are to remain detained at the end of a Tribunal hearing. It is also important to remember that the Tribunal is evaluating the case at the time of the hearing and a decision to discharge a patient from detention is not impugning the original decision to detain.

> ### EXPERT QUOTE
>
> *It is not a question of 'winning' or 'losing' – the issue here is giving evidence as to the statutory criteria.*

Could professionals simply seek to re-detain a patient after a Tribunal decision to discharge? The starting point would be no they could not – because this would undermine a judicial decision and would make rather a mockery of the whole Tribunal proceedings. However, the Courts have recognised that, in mental health work, professionals are dealing with sometimes rapidly changing situations and risks:

CASE STUDY

R (von Brandenburg) v East London and City MH NHS Trust *[2003] UKHL*

Count Von Brandenburg is admitted under s.4 from a homeless hostel and subsequently detained under s.2. He applies to the Tribunal and, at the hearing, a week later, the Tribunal order discharge delayed for one week to allow accommodation to be found. The Tribunal find evidence of mental disorder but do not think detention is justified in the interests of the patient's health, his safety or for the protection of others. The Tribunal say that it is appropriate for accommodation to be found in the community and a care plan be made, including possible medication.

A day before the discharge is to take effect, the patient is detained under s.3 – the medical recommendations record that he is agitated, hostile, delusional, manic, no insight and refusing medication or out-patient care.

The Count challenges the lawfulness of the new detention. The case goes all the way to the House of Lords (what would now be the Supreme Court). The challenge is unsuccessful for many reasons, but the key paragraph from the Lords' judgement is this:

an ASW [*Approved Social Worker – this would now be an Approved Mental Health Professional (AMHP)*] may not lawfully apply for the admission of a patient whose discharge has been ordered by the decision of a Mental Health Review Tribunal of which the ASW is aware unless the ASW has formed the reasonable and bona fide opinion that he has information not known to the Tribunal which puts a significantly different complexion on the case as compared with that which was before the Tribunal.

ACTIVITY *11.1*

Having read the above case example, consider the following question.

- *Can you think of the type of information that might put a significantly different complexion on the case compared with that which was before the Tribunal?*

Complaints

This book has said quite a lot about the expectations on professionals writing reports or attending hearings to give evidence, and it is important to add that anything we have said about professional conduct applies equally to the Panel Members and the legal representative.

Legal representatives' legal and ethical duties are primarily towards their client, i.e. the patient, and to the Court. However, the Mental Health Lawyers Association Code of Conduct includes a requirement that members conduct themselves professionally and courteously. Almost all legal representatives will be Law Society Mental Health Panel Members (otherwise, Legal Aid will not pay for their representation at a hearing) and will usually be employed by a firm of solicitors with a Legal Aid mental health contract. Mental Health Act Administration teams will probably have details of the relevant firm (who must have a clear complaints procedure), so concerns could be raised in the first instance with a senior person at the firm (partner or supervising solicitor).

The Tribunal have mechanisms for raising concerns they may have about hospitals, professionals and legal representatives, but there are also procedures for raising concerns about the Tribunal.

For England:

If the complaint is about an administrative issue, then the relevant agency is HMCTS and you can find details of the procedure here:

www.gov.uk/government/organisations/hm-Courts-and-Tribunals-service/about/complaints-procedure

If the complaint is about 'judicial conduct' which means any member of the Panel, not just the Judge, then this becomes something of a maze in that the Tribunal website directs one to the Judicial Conduct Investigations Office whose website says they do not investigate Tribunal Members but advises complaints should be made to the Tribunal President. The contact details for the President are here:

www.complaints.judicialconduct.gov.uk/Tribunalscomplaints/

The relevant chamber is the Health, Education and Social Care Chamber. There is a three-month time limit for complaints.

For Wales:

Neither the MHRT Wales nor the Welsh Government website have specific details of complaints procedures; however, the general contact details for MHRT Wales are here:

https://mentalhealthreviewTribunal.gov.wales/contact

We would suggest correspondence is for the attention of the President of the MHRT Wales.

Top tips

- *Lawfully detaining a patient again after a Tribunal decision to discharge would require professionals (particularly the AMHP) to show evidence that information has emerged that would have had a material effect on the Tribunal proceedings.*

- *The patient or the Responsible Authority may seek a review of a Tribunal decision or permission to appeal if they feel an error of law has been made.*

- *Tribunals are not won or lost – they are an exercise in independently evaluating competing views about the need for the use of the MHA.*

- *The obligation to conduct oneself courteously and professionally applies to all the professionals involved in the case, including the Panel and the legal representative.*

Chapter summary

- The Tribunal must provide the parties with a written decision and may give an oral decision at the hearing.

- A written decision must be provided within three working days of an s.2 case and within seven days in all other cases.

- There are various ways to challenge a decision depending on the type of mistake that is being asserted.

- Minor mistakes or slips can simply be rectified.

- An obvious error may be dealt with by a review of the decision.

- Challenges claiming an error of law will require an application for permission to appeal.

- If an appeal proceeds it may be dealt with by agreement, by a hearing on the papers or by an oral hearing.

Recommended further reading and online resources

Further reading

For those interested in further legal and procedural detail about the operation of the Tribunal system, the following books are excellent:

Fennell, P, Letts, P and Wilson, J (2013) Mental Health Tribunals: Law, Policy and Practice. London: The Law Society.

Johnston, S, Miles, S and Royston, C (2015) Mental Health Tribunal Handbook. London: Legal Action Group.

For detailed information on Tribunals and the Mental Health Act generally, you will see most Judges and legal representatives carrying a copy of the Mental Health Act Manual:

Jones, R (2020) Mental Health Act Manual, 23rd edn. London: Thomson Reuters.

For detailed information on the complex legal provisions relating to the mental health care of children and young people:

Parker, C (2020) Adolescent Mental Health Care and the Law. London: Legal Action Group.

Not MHT specific but for helpful general guidance on providing both written and oral evidence in Court proceedings:

Seymour, C and Seymour R (2011) Courtroom and Report Writing Skills for Social Workers. London: SAGE.

Online resources

Mental Health Law Online is a comprehensive, free resource for all aspects of mental health law, including Tribunal information:

www.mentalhealthlaw.co.uk

For detailed case-law searches, BAILII is also an excellent free resource:

www.bailii.org

Helpful information, forms, guidance and information for patients can be found on the English and Welsh Government websites:

www.gov.uk/courts-tribunals/first-tier-tribunal-mental-health

And:

mentalhealthreviewtribunal.gov.wales

MIND, Young Minds and the Royal College of Psychiatry have very helpful websites with information for adult and younger patients:

https://youngminds.org.uk/media/2779/youngminds_guide-to-mental-health_v3.pdf

www.mind.org.uk/information-support/legal-rights/leaving-hospital/mental-health-Tribunal/

www.rcpsych.ac.uk/docs/default-source/members/faculties/child-and-adolescent-psychiatry/cap-camhs-guide-to-mental-health-Tribunals-feb-2016.pdf?sfvrsn=cf42b347_2

Glossary of terms and abbreviations

ABH   Actual bodily harm

AC   Approved Clinician as defined in s.145(1) MHA. An additional level of approval required to carry out various functions under the MHA

AMHP   Approved Mental Health Professional

Appointeeship   A process whereby an organisation or individual can apply to be appointed by the Department of Work and Pensions (DWP) to manage an individual's state benefits. www.gov.uk/become-appointee-for-someone-claiming-benefits

AWOL   Absent without leave

CAMHS   Child and Adolescent Mental Health Services

CC   Care Coordinator (called Lead Practitioners in some areas)

CCG   Clinical Commissioning Group

CETR   Care, Education and Treatment Review

Community compulsion   Shorthand for CTOs, Guardianship or conditional discharge. All of which compel the patient to adhere to certain conditions or requirements but none of which can deprive the patient of their liberty

Community patient   A patient subject to a Community Treatment Order (s.145(2)). A CTO places the patient under certain conditions in the community

CPA   Care Programme Approach (England) although used in the Practice Direction to refer more generically to Care 'Pathway' – which could be any specific pathway such as WRAP or CETP

CQC   Care Quality Commission

CTP   Care and Treatment Plan – places duties on care coordinators in Wales to prepare, consult and review these plans with the relevant patients

DHSC   Department of Health and Social Care

DoLS   Deprivation of Liberty Safeguards

Duties   a legal obligation or requirement, commonly referred to as a 'must do'

ECHR   European Convention on Human Rights. The full title is the European Convention for the Protection of Human Rights and Fundamental Freedoms

ECtHR   European Court of Human Rights

ESR   Extra-statutory recommendations. Sometimes requested in restricted cases where the Tribunal has no power to make statutory recommendations about matters such as leave or transfer. ESRs have no legal force but might be persuasive

Guardianship   Under s.7 or s.37, a patient received into Guardianship may need to adhere to certain requirements

Guidance   MHA Codes explain this as a 'should do' and with reference to the MHA and MCA Codes of Practice, both are statutory guidance which the relevant professionals must 'have regard to'

HMH   Hospital Managers Hearings or reviews. Hospital Managers have the power to discharge certain patients from detention or CTOs. The requirement to hold reviews of patients' cases is undertaken by a group of at least three people not employed by the hospital

HRA   Human Rights Act 1998

IMHA   Independent Mental Health Advocate

LA   Local Authority sometimes also referred to as the Local Social Services Authority

Legal Aid   Government funding for legal advice and services. Legal representation in Tribunal proceedings is non-means-tested, which means there is no cost to the patient. Legal Aid is available for other work such as representation at Hospital Managers Hearings, but this funding is means-tested

LHB   Local Health Board. The equivalent to a CCG in Wales

LPA   Lasting Power of Attorney as defined in s.9 of the Mental Capacity Act

LPS   Liberty Protection Safeguards. An informal term for the Mental Capacity (Amendment) Act 2019 which will replace the current Deprivation of Liberty Safeguards when in force

MAPPA   Multi-Agency Public Protection Panel. www.gov.uk/government/publications/channel-and-prevent-multi-agency-Panel-pmap-guidance

MARAC   Multi-Agency Risk Assessment Conference

MCA   Mental Capacity Act 2005

Measures   Law applying only to Wales

Mental disorder   Any disorder or disability of the mind (s.1 MHA)

MHA   Mental Health Act 1983

MHA Code   Code of Practice to the Mental Health Act. English Code 2015 and Welsh Code 2016

MHAA or MHAO   Mental Health Act Administrator or Mental Health Act Office. The Administrative team will manage all the necessary stages of ensuring patients are aware of their rights, managing applications and references to the Tribunal and coordinating with the Tribunal Office. The MHA Admin team in a hospital will undertake many of the duties of the Hospital Managers and are responsible for a wide range of requirements related to the MHA. Sometimes known as MHA Law departments

MHRTW   Mental Health Review Tribunal for Wales

MHT   Mental Health Tribunal (England)

MM   Medical Member of the Tribunal Panel

MoJ   Ministry of Justice. Restricted patients all have a caseworker within the Mental Health Casework Unit of the MoJ

NICE   National Institute for Health and Care Excellence

NR   Nearest relative. A specific role in the MHA as set out in s.26–s.28. The NR has a number of important rights and powers

OT   Occupational therapist

Part II, III, IV, etc. MHA   The Mental Health Act is set out in Parts. The key parts for the purposes of this book are Part II civil admissions; Part III patients concerned in criminal proceedings or under sentence; Part IV consent to treatment and Part V Tribunals

Patient   A person suffering or appearing to be suffering from mental disorder (s.145(4) MHA)

PD   Practice Direction. Detailed guidance expanding on the Tribunal Rules. The most relevant being the PDs in relation to statements and reports in Tribunal cases

PHE   Pre-hearing examination – an examination of the patient by the Medical Member ahead of a hearing

PMAP   Channel and Prevent Multi-Agency Panel

Powers   Legal authority given to a person or body to undertake specific functions, commonly referred to as a 'could or can do'

PRN Medication   Refers to the Latin phrase pro re nata meaning 'as required'. Often asked about in Tribunal hearings because frequent PRN use might indicate the patient experiencing a high level of distress or agitation

RC   Responsible Clinician. This is defined in s.34 MHA as being the Approved Clinician with overall responsibility for the patient's case. This is usually, but not always, a psychiatrist. It could be a clinical psychologist or social worker with the required approval

SCR   Social Circumstances Report the requirements of which are set out in the Practice Direction

Section 117   Sometimes referred to as s.117 aftercare. A section of the MHA that applies to certain patients and places a duty on the relevant Health and Local Authority bodies to arrange for and/or provide aftercare

Section 17 leave   The section of the MHA that sets out the powers of the RC (and Secretary of State/Welsh Ministers) to grant leave from hospital to certain patients

SpLM   Specialist Lay Member of the Tribunal Panel. Wales use the phrase Lay Members. We use the abbreviation SpLM to refer to both

Tribunal   We use this shorthand to apply to both the English and Welsh Tribunal systems

UKUT   UK Upper Tribunal. The Upper Tribunal hear appeals from both the English and Welsh Tribunals

Table of cases

AF v Nottinghamshire NHS Trust [2015] UKUT 216

AMA v Greater Manchester West Mental Health NHS Foundation Trust [2015] UKUT 36

C v Birmingham and Solihull Mental Health NHS Trust [2013] EWCA Civ 701

CNWL NHS Foundation Trust v H-JH [2012] UKUT 210

Djaba v West London Mental Health Trust [2017] EWCA Civ 436

Dorset Healthcare NHS Foundation Trust v MH [2009] UKUT 4

JLG v Managers of Llanarth Court [2011] UKUT 62

MA v SSH [2012] UKUT 474

MC v Cygnet Behavioural Health Ltd and Secretary of State for Justice [2020] UKUT 230 (AAC)

MH v UK [2013] ECHR 1008

Porter v Magill [2002] 2AC 357

R (RD) v MHRT [2007] EWHC 781 Admin

R v East London and the City Mental Health Trust Ex p Brandenburg [2003] UKHL 58

R(H) v Ashworth Hospital Authority [2002] EWCA Civ 923

R(H) v MHRT for the Mersey Regional Health Authority [1986] 1 WLR 1170

R(H) v SSH [2006] 1 AC 44

R(on the application of AN) v MHRT [2005] EWHC 587 (Admin)

R(on the Application of Li) v MHRT [2004] EWHC 51

R(on the application of SC) v Mental Health Review Tribunal and the Secretary of State for Health [2005] EWHC 17

R (on the application of von Brandenburg) v East London and City MH NHS Trust [2003] UKHL 58

RB v Nottinghamshire Healthcare NHS Trust [2011] UKUT 73

RM v St Andrew's Healthcare [2010] UKUT 119 (AAC)

Re AB (Inherent Jurisdiction: Deprivation of Liberty) [2018] EWHC 3103 (Fam)

Re Ian Brady [2011] First-tier Tribunal 7 December 2011

Secretary of State for Justice v MM [2018] UKSC 60

SH v Cornwall Partnership NHS Trust [2012] UKUT 290

SL v Ludlow Street Healthcare [2015] UKUT 398 (AAC)

SM v Livewell Southwest CIC [2020] UKUT 191 (AAC)

South Staffordshire and Shropshire Healthcare NHS Foundation Trust v The Hospital Managers of St George's Hospital [2016] EWHC 1196

SSJ v MM [2017] EWCA Civ 194

VS v St. Andrew's Healthcare [2018] UKUT 250

Welsh Ministers v PJ [2018] UKSC 66

YA v CNWL NHS TRUST and Others [2015] UKUT 37 (AAC)

Table of legislation, statutory materials and guidance

Additional Learning Needs and Educational Tribunal (Wales) Act 2018

Care Act 2014

Care and Treatment Review: Policy and Guidance 2015

Children Act 1989

Children Act 2004

Children and Families Act 2014

Children (Leaving Care) Act 2000

Code of Practice to Parts 2 and 3 of the Mental Health (Wales) Measure 2010

[The] Courts and Tribunal Service: Reports for Mental Health Tribunals 2012

Department of Health and Social Care (2021) Reforming the Mental Health Act

Domestic Violence, Crime and Victims Act 2004

European Convention for the Protection of Human Rights and Fundamental Freedoms 1950

Guidance for the Observation of Tribunal Hearings in the First-tier Tribunal Health Education and Social Care Chamber (Mental Health Jurisdiction) 10 January 2019

HMCTS Minimum Requirements for Tribunal Hearings to be Held in Hospitals. April 2018

Human Right Act 1998

[The] Law Society: Representation before Mental Health Tribunals. Practice Note 2019

Legal Aid Act 1949

Lunacy Act 1890

Magna Carta 1215

Mental Capacity Act 2005

Mental Capacity Amendment Act 2019 (commonly termed the 'Liberty Protection Safeguards')

Mental Health (Approval of Persons to be Approved Mental Health Professionals) (Wales) Regulations 2008

Mental Health (Approved Mental Health Professionals) (Approval) (England) Regulations 2008

Mental Health (Hospital) (England) Regulations 2008

Mental Health (Hospital, Guardianship, Community Treatment and Consent to Treatment) (Wales) Regulations 2008

Mental Health Act 1959

Mental Health Act 1983

Mental Health Act 2007

Mental Health Act 1983 Code of Practice 2015

Mental Health Act 1983 Code of Practice for Wales

[The] Mental Health (Approved Mental Health Professionals) (Approval) (England) Regulations 2008

[The] Mental Health (Approval of Persons to be Approved Mental Health Professionals) (Wales) Regulations 2008)

Mental Health Act 1983 (Remedial Order) 2001 (SI 2001/3712)

Mental Health Review Tribunal for Wales Practice Direction: Statements and Reports for Mental Health Review Tribunals in Wales 2019

Mental Health Review Tribunal for Wales Rules 2008

Mental Health (Wales) Measure 2010

Mental Treatment Act 1930

Multi-Agency Public Protection Arrangements. May 2021

National Health Service Act 2006 (England) Approved Clinician (General) Directions 2008

National Health Service Wales Mental Health Act 1983 (Approved Clinicians) (Wales) Directions 2018

NHS England. (2017) Care and Treatment Review: Policy and Guidance

Practice Direction First-tier Tribunal: Statements and Reports in Mental Health Cases 2013

Practice Guidance on Procedures Concerning Handling Representations from Victims in the First-tier Tribunal (Mental Health) 2011

Practice Note: Role of the Independent Mental Health Advocate in First-tier Tribunal (Mental Health) Hearings 2011

Practice Statement: Composition of Tribunals in relation to Matters That Fall to be Decided by the Health, Education and Social Care Chamber on or after 16 December 2015

Reference Guide to the Mental Health Act 1983

Reforming the Mental Health Act – White Paper (Department of Health and Social Care, 2021)

Rights of Children and Young People (Wales) Measure 2011

[The] Role of the Independent Mental Health Advocate in First-tier Tribunal (Mental Health) Hearings. May 2011

Section 67 of the Mental Health Act 1983: References by the Secretary of State for Health and Social Care to the First-tier Tribunal. August 2019

Social Services and Wellbeing (Wales) Act 2014

Tribunal Procedure (First-tier Tribunal) (Health, Education and Social Care Chamber) Rules 2008

Tribunals, Courts and Enforcement Act 2007

United Nations Convention on the Rights of the Child 1990

Bibliography

Allen, N (citing Diesfield) (2009) Journal of Mental Health Law (Winter 2009). Northumbria: Northumbria Law Press.

Barber, P, Brown, R and Martin, D (2019) Mental Health Law in England and Wales, 4th edn. London: SAGE.

Bartlett, P and Sandland, R (2007) Mental Health Law Policy and Practice, 4th edn. Oxford: OUP.

Brown, R. (2020) The Approved Mental Health Professional's Guide to Mental Health Law, 5th edn. London: SAGE.

Care Quality Commission (2017) Monitoring the Mental Health Act 2016–2017. Newcastle: CQC.

Care Quality Commission (2018) Monitoring the Mental Health Act 2017–2018. Newcastle: CQC.

Care Quality Commission and Administrative Justice and Tribunals Council (2011) Patients Experiences of the First-tier Tribunal (Mental Health). Newcastle: CQC.

Fennell, P, Letts, P and Wilson, J. (2013) Mental Health Tribunals: Law, Policy and Practice. London: The Law Society.

Gostin, L, Bartlett, P, Fennell, P, McHale, J and Mackay, R (eds) (2010) Principles of Mental Health Law and Policy. Oxford: OUP.

Hale, B (2017) Mental Health Law, 6th edn. London: Sweet & Maxwell.

Hutchison, C and Hickman, N (2016) Focus on Social Work Law: Mental Health. London: Palgrave McMillan.

Jacobs, E (2011) Tribunal Practice and Procedure: Tribunals under the Tribunals, Courts and Enforcement Act 2007, 2nd edn. London: Legal Action Group.

Jones, R (2020) Mental Health Act Manual, 23rd edn. London: Thomson Reuters.

Tribunal System (Senior President of Tribunals' Annual Report 2020)

Index

Locators in **bold** refer to tables and those in *italics* to figures.